# STUCK IN STUPID

## A CORNWALL LEGEND'S LIFE IN THE FAST LANE

### BRIAN "THE CAT" ROULEAU
ANDY PETEPIECE

Tellwell Talent
www.tellwell.ca

ISBN
978-1-998454-17-4 (Paperback)
978-1-998454-18-1 (eBook)

# ACKNOWLEDGMENTS

To my wonderful daughters Jessica Ann Parsons and Michelle Rouleau who stuck by me through thick and thin and my handsome grandson Finn and beautiful granddaughter Callie. I dedicate this book to you so, that someday you can look back and smile and always remember your father and grandfather "The Cat."

The lesson I want you to learn is …It doesn't matter what you look like, you can be tall short fat thin ugly, or handsome like your father, or you can be black or yellow or white, it's irrelevant. Of most importance is the size of your heart and the strength of your character.

Herman Munster (Brian Rouleau)

To the Rouleau Boys
Tom Good, Rick Kalil, Bear Lalonde, John Dickey, Claude McIntosh, Larry Gabri, and Andy Petepiece

To the late great Bob Megenhardt
You are missed by everyone who knew you, especially me.

To John "Johnny G" Gallinger

My Friend for life

To Byron Gallinger
A loyal friend for 65 years

To Billy Phillips
My full-time Canadian sidekick

To Duncan Black
My Limelight Atlanta main man

To Guy D'Alema
Photographer to the Stars

To Al Whitton
A man among men

To Billy Ingram
The man at the top of the mountain

To Joe McFall
My bodyguard while on tour

To Stu Stone
My New York connection

To Ron Begg
Host of "I Begg Your Pardon"

To Claude MacIntosh
Grateful for the years of support

To Julie MacIntosh
One of the best

A very special shout out and thanks to all my friends and relatives who stood by me and helped me overcome activities that would have to be classified.

## "STUCK IN STUPID"

# INTRODUCTION

I always liked being noticed. But, as a youth, I didn't achieve gratification with my academic or sports skills. I didn't have the ambition, the desire to become a bookworm, or the patience to deal with all the sports jocks because I didn't appreciate that crowd.

I would draw attention to myself by acting up and being the class pest. Unfortunately, my inner anger or desire to be protective of others got me into many altercations and made me stand out. So then, the Sea Cadets came along, and I loved their uniforms, the band, and the many public demonstrations we performed.

Also, I served three tours during my Vietnam era and got little positive recognition. Still, at least being back home in Canada, I thought I looked sharp in my dress uniform, and the fact that I served in combat in Vietnam created notice.

When I was involved in the nightclub business, it was terrific to be a part of an exciting, attention-drawing milieu. Being involved with many celebrities who visited our clubs, partaking in informative conversations, and having my picture taken with them suited me just perfectly.

I have always dressed to the nines and worn lots of expensive bling. These are not the practices of someone wanting to be shy. My cars were always top-of-the-line Mercedes, Cadillacs, Lincolns, and brand-new Limousines. I often had convertibles because I wished the people to know "The Cat's in Town," and now I have stickers on my present car indicating my military service. A little self-indulgence, for sure.

Writing this book is more of the same. I want readers to know about my life. It would be foolish to pretend I didn't want to stand out. It is so evident in my look and behavior. Does this attention-seeking make me a bad person? I don't think so. My ego is in check. I am often self-deprecating, and my buddies tease me mercilessly. My need to be noticed stems from my low self-esteem as a youngster due to my life without money, good clothes, and a decent home.

I have decided to write my life story as honestly as possible. You can't count the number of poor decisions I've made, big and small. Stuck in Stupid was prevalent during my early years, but there is no point in criticizing my former wives and some business associates.

Failure usually has two partners, and I refuse to engage in bitterness publicly. That doesn't mean I will ignore some people in my past, but I hope to give an honest opinion where clarification is needed. Instead, I need to address them so readers will better understand me. The same is true for some business conflicts. But, again, I will describe them fairly and honestly.

Finally, I am excited about this project. I am reconnecting with many old friends as we seek their stories about our lives together. These conversations have produced a lot of laughs and tears but an overwhelming feeling of being incredibly lucky to have such a large support group. So, I am throwing my life open to scrutiny to gain recognition and a sense of accomplishment. I hope that many of you will enjoy reading about my life.

I have zero expectations of making money on this project, and I have no hidden ideas of ever obtaining any recognition from the Pulitzer Prize people. Most say I will be lucky to break even as I self-publish this book which means money is going out and not in. Ah well. (Big smile)

# TABLE OF CONTENTS

ACKNOWLEDGMENTS . . . . . . . . . . . . . . . . . . . . . . . . . . . . V

INTRODUCTION . . . . . . . . . . . . . . . . . . . . . . . . . VII

CHAPTER 1: MY EARLY YEARS . . . . . . . . . . . . . . . . . . . . . . 2

CHAPTER 2: SIGNING UP WITH UNCLE SAM . . . . . . . . 16

CHAPTER 3: IN COUNTRY . . . . . . . . . . . . . . . . . . . . . . . 31

CHAPTER 4: MY DISCO ERA BEGINS . . . . . . . . . . . . . . . 47

CHAPTER 5: THE LIMELIGHT IN HALLANDALE
           FLORIDA . . . . . . . . . . . . . . . . . . . . . . . . . . . . . .66

CHAPTER 6: THE ATLANTA LIMELIGHT
           1979-1984 . . . . . . . . . . . . . . . . . . . . . . . . . . . . .77

CHAPTER 7: THE ATLANTA ADULT CLUB YEARS . . . .93

CHAPTER 8: ADULT ENTERTAINMENT IN
           TAMPA FLORIDA . . . . . . . . . . . . . . . . . . . . . .101

CHAPTER 9: THE BIG EASY . . . . . . . . . . . . . . . . . . . . . . .106

CHAPTER 10: ROULEAU STORIES ONE . . . . . . . . . . . . . .112

CHAPTER 11: ROULEAU STORIES TWO . . . . . . . . . . . . . .122

REFLECTIONS. . . . . . . . . . . . . . . . . . . . . . . . . . . . . . . . . . . . .129

APPENDIX A: SOME OF BRIAN'S FRIENDS . . . . . . . . .131

APPENDIX B: SOME OF BRIAN'S VEHICLES . . . . . . . .135

APPENDIX C: CORNWALL AREA VIETNAM VETS . . .137

APPENDIX D: CELEBRITIES I MET. . . . . . . . . . . . . . . . .138

# CHAPTER ONE

## MY EARLY YEARS

Cornwall is located along the mighty Saint Lawrence River, where the provinces of Ontario and Quebec and the state of New York converge. It shares its southern border with the Mohawk Nation of Akwesasne.

Originally named New Johnstown, my hometown changed its name to Cornwall in honor of Prince George, The Duke of Cornwall. It was incorporated as a town in 1834 and became a city in 1945. That was the year Brian "The Cat" Rouleau arrived with the sound of thunder.

### MEMORIES OF DOWNTOWN CORNWALL

Growing up in Cornwall was an exciting and wonderful experience, with some of the largest industrial companies in eastern Ontario belching out a wide assortment of pollutants that would never be allowed to operate under the "Green New Deal" of this day and age. We weren't worried about the threat of dying from the stuff flying out of the smokestacks and being poured out of the back door drainage systems from the mills directly into the Saint Lawrence because it was 'Boom Time in the City".

Major employers such as The Howard Smith Paper Mill (Later known as Domtar), Courtaulds, and the Cotton Mill kept the city humming with steady jobs and salaries well above the normal. It was a good time to live in the city.

Who couldn't remember the thrill of walking down Pitt Street in the '50s and '60s to the sounds of rock & roll blasting from the open windows of the juiced-up automobiles with long radio antennas that looked like fishing rods at Gray's Creek. On Friday nights, the crowd was so thick at the bandstand set up in front of the New York Cafe that you had to walk sideways. The sights and sounds were sensational, and I loved it!

Each store had neon lights blazing out its name. I recall Levesque, a baby store, Tamblyn's Drug Store, and Woolworths. The latter sold miniature turtles you could slide into your pocket without anyone knowing. I accumulated about a dozen "playmates" until my mother found them wandering about my bedroom. She forced me to return the turtles to the store and explain what I had done to the manager. I had acted like an outlaw, and this was the beginning of my life of being "Stuck in Stupid."

## ENTERTAINMENT

Other memories include the Zellers store with the electric riding horse at the front entrance. I could ride my heart out for a nickel and fantasize about being on the range alongside Roy Rodgers and Dale Evans. I loved the Palace movie theater, and the Capital, with its magnificent architectural design and excellent balcony. From there, my buddies and I would terrorize the unsuspecting crowd below by bombarding them with empty popcorn boxes or using straws to fire kernels at their heads.

Some of my favorite movies included; the Three Stooges, King Kong, the Monster from the Black Lagoon, and Bella Lugosi starring in Dracula. The top cartoons were Bugs Bunny, Sylvester the Cat, Donald Duck, and Popeye. It was a special treat to watch some of these shows at the Roxy Theater in Cornwall's east end. They had the best popcorn in town, always fresh out of the popper.

## THE YOUNG ENTREPRENEUR

My mother never had the money for things like the movies, so I had a choice, either I get out and find some odd jobs or not be able to attend the shows with my friends. So consequently, I began picking up empty soft drink bottles and turning them in for a penny a bottle, cutting grass for a couple of bucks with a lawn mower that was noiseless except for my grunting. I was the engine! Remember those?

Shoveling snow door to door all over the city in blistering snowstorms was a challenge. I would wear running shoes with hockey socks pulled over them because we couldn't afford snow boots. The icy wind would reach through our thin windbreakers like the fingers of Frosty the Snowman. But, with teeth chattering, fingers frozen, and feet so cold, we had problems walking. I would place pieces of cardboard in my running shoes because of the worn-out soles. I could step on a dime and tell you whether it was heads or tails. We never gave up. It just wasn't an option.

## A TERRIFIC CHRISTMAS MEMORY

I remember one Christmas, my mother sat me down with tears in her eyes and told me that she couldn't afford to buy Christmas presents, and I started to cry. Of course, being a young kid and knowing the circumstances, I understood, but it didn't make me feel any better.

About a half hour later, I heard this stomp stomp stomp sound of heavy boots walking up the stairs and heading towards our apartment. Bang! Bang! Bang! Someone was knocking on our door. Who could that be at this time of the night, I wondered,

I gingerly opened the door, and two huge men dressed in uniforms stood looking down at me. My first thought was, "Oh, oh! What did they find out that I did this time?" Thankfully it wasn't the cops but two men from the Cornwall Fire Department. One of the men shouted, "Merry Christmas!" I was startled and surprised.

Out from behind their backs, they pulled a large box the size of a big trunk. It contained a fantastic collection of toys and clothes. The fireman said we heard that times were tough this Christmas, and we wanted you to have something special this year. My mother started crying, I was smiling and laughing from ear to ear, and the firemen were beaming like the North Star. I will never forget the kindness that Christmas Eve. Both of those firemen will always be in my heart, especially around the Christmas holidays.

## SHOE SHINE BOY

Snetsinger's Hardware on Pitt Street was located beside the New York Cafe and directly across the street from our small upstairs apartment.

When Snetsinger's was closed for the day in the summer, I would set up my little shoeshine box and solicit anyone walking by with a cheerful "Would you like a shine, Mr.?" I charged a quarter for the best shine in town (at least

I thought so). Business was so good that I let the customer read one of my comic books for free and charged them five cents for a glass of lemonade. Hell of a deal, "The Cat" was on his way to becoming an entrepreneur and, as famous civil rights activist Jessie Jackson used to say, being a "Somebody."

## WORKING THE MILK ROUTE

I am not proud of my "work" as a helper on an East Side Dairy wagon delivering milk door to door. Unfortunately, as I did my rounds, I learned that the trusting public put money in the empty milk bottles outside their doors, often with a brief note indicating what products they required. This money was the mother lode, and it wasn't long before I did my own "rounds" very early in the morning. Later, after trudging up to the door to deliver the milk, I would return to the driver faking puzzlement as to why there was no money in the bottles. As you can imagine, it didn't take East Side Dairy long to figure out what was happening. As a result, my "employment" with them quickly ended.

Life was poor, but life was great, and I was getting wild and crazy. With a pocket full of coins and a smile, I felt that my most fantastic dreams seemed possible for a fleeting moment.

## THE RINK RAT DAYS

We moved from 142 Pitt Street to living on the corner of Amelia and Water Street. I was just about half a block from the Water Street Arena.

One day I decided to go and see if they would put me on as a Rink Rat, a group of kids on skates who scraped the ice. I was just a skinny little guy, and the manager wasn't sure if I was up for the job, but I did a lot of jive-talking, and he told me to report for work the next night.

The Rink Rat's job was sometimes challenging but always exciting and fun. I helped sell stuff from the snack bar and would enthusiastically wander through the crowd hollering "Peanuts, Popcorn, Potato Chips" until someone would yell back the item they wanted. Then, without any hesitation, the requested snack would be jet-propelled in the direction of the request, and a chain of hands passed the money to me so I could move on down the aisle. I am trying to remember the money I received for this magnificent display of marksmanship, but the reward was in the satisfaction that I was the show of the moment for each snack delivery.

The Rink Rat's job was to scrape the ice between periods in preparation for the mighty Zamboni machine to circle with a fresh coat of hot water. We turned the job into our own Super Bowl halftime show. We were on the ice trying to get the crowd's attention, and we knew they were watching our every move. So we lined up in a precision military-style formation and manicured the ice. We did it with confidence and panache. We incorporated our in-between period performance with all the twists and turns of a well-coordinated and choreographed Broadway production.

I remember many of the old Rink Rats; Bobby Jodoin, Ronnie Price, Peter Fishwick, Paul Tremblay, Bordy Harrington, Cecil Shaffer, and Bobby McDermid, who all lived or hung out on Bergen Avenue in the east end of the city. What a bunch!

## BIG TIME WRESTLING

We were also required to set up the chairs around the ring for the then-popular weekly wrestling matches. It was fun to watch the crowd's response when the wrestlers entered. They would erupt with boisterous hoots and hollers depending on whether the incoming wrestler was their favorite or a nasty villain.

Among the wrestlers I recall were; Lou Thesz, a tough and gifted performer; Edward Carpentier, the Flying Frenchman; Gene Kiniski, Canada's Greatest Athlete; and Joe Leduc, the most fantastic heel of all time; and scary, vicious Mad Dog Vachon. Who could forget the tremendous midget wrestlers; Sky Low Low, Fuzzy Cupid, and Little Beaver?

I still find it amazing that most of the crowd didn't seem to know that the wrestlers who appeared to be trying to kill each other all arrived and departed together. They were performers putting on a show, not actual combatants. These matches were great fun to watch.

## RINK RAT INSIDE JOB

Only the inside crew knew about some benefits of the Rink Rat job. For example, during the hockey season, the big soft drink company trucks would pull up beside the arena and park. The drivers would go in and play hockey while we figured it was a good time to check out the product on the truck. But, of course, we enjoyed our spoils and figured no one would miss the odd case of drinks.

Never a group to take advantage of a situation (Ya right, eh!), we only took enough drinks to last until the next truck arrived a few days later.

Yes, I know, this behavior was another reason for me to wind up in hell, but after all, I was "The Cat," not a chicken. Unfortunately, Stuck in Stupid was once again showing its ugly head.

## THE HOCKEY POOL

One more tidbit about the boys at the arena. Every week, the Rink Rats would have what is known as a "Pool" consisting of picking a number that you thought would be the number of goals scored in the Cornwall Chevies game. We charged a quarter a ticket with the promise of winning a pretty good-sized pot. Unfortunately, I don't know what happened, but no one would ever win the pool! Guess why! For those who bought tickets way back then, I say, "Thank you from the bottom of our hearts. You're the best."

The arena was our place, and we did some wild and crazy things. Fortunately, most outsiders have yet to realize what went on behind the walls of the arena. For example, one of the after-hours games was turning the heat up in the dressing rooms high, and each guy would place a bar of soap on the register. Then, we'd turn out the lights and close the door.

We would wait about ten minutes, burst into the room, and turn the lights on. Then, each guy would grab his soap bar and see how many cockroaches he could kill. This activity was an excellent way to spend a couple of minutes daily.

The one with the least number of cockroaches would have to go down to Ma Lalonde's hamburger joint on Pitt and Seventh Street and buy about ten dollars' worth of her famous smothered with onions, ten cent hamburgers and bring them back to the arena for the boys.

Being Stuck in Stupid, it didn't take much to make us happy.

## THE COCA-COLA AFFAIR

Another of our many little escapades required us to visit the Coke Company on Amelia Street after hours when only the night shift would be on duty. The employees' lounge vending machine pumped out cold Cokes for only a penny. We would send a few guys in there to scout out the location of the workers. Then, at an all-clear signal, the rest of us would rush in, and each of us would grab a wooden case of 24 Cokes and beat it down the street to our sanctuary in Central Park.

One night, I was stationed at the door, got the signal, grabbed the case of coke, and ran out the door. About 15 seconds later, I heard this thump thump thump noise, so I looked around and saw this massive guy in a Coke uniform chasing me through about two feet of snow and gaining ground rapidly.

I got about a block away and headed into Central Park, trying to do about 99 miles an hour. Then, finally, I started tossing handfuls of Coke bottles onto the path. But he was not stopping nor slowing down. So finally, with the tension rising and my legs freezing, I ditched the case in his way. He was so close I could feel the heat of his breath, but suddenly he slipped. I had escaped and hurried into the darkness like Batman returning to Gotham City.

From a distance, I could hear the faint sounds of him calling out something like, "The next time, I am going to catch you and kick your ass LB" I didn't know he knew my name, but later I heard he wasn't calling me LB for "Little Brian." The "LB" was for "Little Bastard." He was a little angry with me. We had all made it home safely, not a scratch or a bruise. Once again, we had survived.

I used to have to pass in front of the Coke Company to get to school, so I always faced directly ahead and tried my best to blend in with the snow. In addition, I pulled my toque down tightly so this guy couldn't identify me. If necessary, I would have worn a burlap bag over my head and down to my knees to avoid detection.

## MUSIC

I was really into music and had visions of becoming an entertainer. But unfortunately, I couldn't sing, but I learned to play the drums and the trumpet. I would practice for hours until my fingers would start to bleed, and my lips would get so big I looked like the back end of a buffalo's ass.

I spent every night with a small transistor radio tucked under the covers in my bed, listening to WABC New York radio powerhouse Bruce Morrow better known as "Cousin Brucie," and his Saturday night Rock 'n Roll Party. I'd also tune in to WLS Chicago and "The Wild Italian" Dick Biondi. He was known for his screaming delivery and wild antics on the air. And who could ever forget Robert Weston Smith, professionally known as Wolfman Jack, an American disc jockey famous for his gravelly voice. He credited it for his success, saying, "It's kept meat and potatoes on the table for years, and a couple of shots of whisky helps it."

I dreamt about being on one of their shows and belting out the best in rock n roll on stage, a screaming band behind me and the spotlight blazing away, illuminating my every move. I practiced all the dance steps from the most significant groups of Motown. I hoped to meet Barry Gordy III someday. The world knew Gordy as an American record executive and producer of songs, movies, and TV. He was/is best known as the founder of the Motown record label. Gordy could give me a pass about lack of talent but credit me with an overabundance of desire. And that, my friends, is what dreaming is all about.

## MIDNIGHT SWIMMING

I lived at the corner of Amelia and Water Street, directly across from Central Park and the city-owned pool. The fence wasn't a problem, for we'd climb it like the young monkeys we were. But, of course, we'd have to keep a keen eye out for the local constables who frequently drove past. When they did, we'd hug the pool's edges, becoming nearly invisible.

## THE ICE HOUSE

The ice house was just about a half block from my home. Men cut slabs of ice from the St. Lawrence and stored them in the facility. Then the workers cut them into smaller pieces which they delivered to homes for non-ice-making refrigerators. We used to walk in and help ourselves to the slivers of ice that broke off from the main slabs. They were the only popsicles we could afford, with no flavor, but they did the job.

## MY FATHER

I first met my father when I was four years old. He was a stranger to me and an upsetting presence that day. He decided to take me to a local clothing store called "Dover's" and had them outfit me with a little suit. Next, he dropped me off at my grandmother's and disappeared.

I never saw him again.

My dad did phone once when I was home on leave between my second and third tours of Vietnam. When I picked up the phone, I heard, "Is that you, son?" Irritated, I replied, "Sorry, you have the wrong number," and hung up. My mother was not too pleased with my response, but to me, he was no father of mine.

Years later, someone told me some stories about my father. First of all, he was known as a scrapper with a short fuse and was not to be trifled with if you had a few beers. Secondly, I learned that officers from Cornwall Police picked him up at my grandmother's house on Third Street for failing to meet his support payments. They had to drag him around the corner to the police station on Pitt Street, for they couldn't get him into the police cruiser. Finally, when I heard this story as an adult, I was not surprised by the charge.

## MY MOM

It is fair to say we were poor. Our home was a dingy apartment on the upper level of a Pitt Street commercial building. Mom was short and thin but always tried to create a positive atmosphere. I was lucky because she demonstrated much love toward me, which benefited me my entire life.

Mom, born Edna Martel, eked out a living waiting tables in a restaurant on Pitt Street called the "Chicken Palace" and saved every nickel she could. When I did well financially in later years, I would send money to give her a better life. For example, one time when I was home visiting, mom complained about her fridge freezing over. Upon inspection, I found stacks of hundred-dollar bills I had sent her frozen solid in the freezer. She never spent the money on herself but squirreled it away.

Unfortunately, when I was young, my mom hooked up with a loser who often beat me. Frank McAvoy was out of Port Hope, Ontario. We lived directly across the street from the New York Café, and this mutt used to take great pride in opening the front window and urinating on Pitt Street. Stupid things like that were daily occurrences with him every time he was drunk. These juvenile acts were his way of showing the world that he didn't give a damn about what anyone thought of him.

This mutt enjoyed pounding me up just a little too much for my liking. As I grew older and more robust, the fights became less one-sided. One day we nearly destroyed the apartment in a wild battle that included throwing him down thirty stairs to the street below while I beat the living hell out of him all the way. We landed in the middle of Pitt Street with my hands securely wrapped snugly around his neck and the local cops trying to pry me loose. It looked like a wrestling match in Madison Square Gardens, but this was for real.

The cops finally broke up the fight and told me I was lucky I hadn't killed him. I retorted, "Too bad I didn't; it would have been my pleasure." The Crown Attorney didn't lay any charges, but the officers warned me to go home and cool off. Thanks, boys; I love you too.

Years later, I was happy to learn my dad was dying of cancer. But unfortunately, his constant violence was a significant contributor to my rebelliousness.

## MY SIBLINGS

I have a sister, Joan, who served in the Canadian Air Force. She was quite a bit older and had left home when I was very young. I got along well with Joan, who spent a lot of time trying to keep me on the right path. To this day, I greatly appreciate her efforts. Joan passed away in December of 2024.

Pat was my older brother, named after my father. He went by the label of "Jr." He was a big man, well-built and strong, and I hoped to be able to run with him as I got older, but for some reason, we didn't get along.

Pat left home to join the military and was a member of Princess Patricia's Canadian Light Infantry, an elite part of the Canadian Army. I used to brag to my friends that I was very impressed with his time in the service, but I quietly resented not having a brother by my side like my friends.

On one of his home visits, we got into a knock-down drag-out fight. I was watching a TV program, and Pat was ready to eat dinner. Aggressively he yelled at me to "get to the kitchen table and eat!" I replied, "I will be right there in a minute" I guess my response wasn't what he wanted to hear, and he got up from the table, walked up behind me, and cuffed me upside my head.

I came out of the chair doing about a hundred miles an hour. The door to the oven was open, and we fell and broke the door off the hinges. I tried to knock him out with a chair, and then we wrestled into the hall, down the stairs landing on Amelia Street, and then into the park.

My mother was screaming, my sister was crying, and I was swinging like a buzz-saw out of hell. I had had enough of having people putting their hands on me. I vowed that day that I would never allow an assault to happen again without retaliating immediately. The cops became involved, and it was a mess. That fiasco was in the 1960s. We reconciled on his deathbed in December of 2024.

## CLOTHING

My good friend Andy Petepiece recently asked me about my clothing situation because we were so poor. I explained what little I had was from the Salvation Army or one of the local pawn shops on First Street.

I told Andy that my lack of "standard" clothes made me feel insecure, and you can see that reflected in my clothing when I got money. I always buy the best shoes and apparel and lots of bling. Although everyone might not like my taste, these purchases add to my feeling of security and demonstrate that I am no longer poor.

## SCHOOL DAYS

Many of my friends came from low-income families, so I didn't always feel uncomfortable. However, the change came when I was at school, and it was obvious that most of the other students were better dressed and fed. Suddenly I felt like an outsider; I felt like I was in the wrong place. Sometimes, if it rained, I would escape school by deliberately getting soaking wet and covered with mud. Then, I would seek permission to go home and change with no intention of returning until the next day. Some of my teachers were just as glad to be rid of me.

## MISS JENNIE CAROTHERS

I recall one strict female teacher who developed a soft spot in her hard heart for me. I vividly remember spending more time sitting on the coat room floor, banned from the class for being a little pain in the ass. However, Miss Jennie Carothers loved to play golf and decided to give poor Brian some insight into a better life by having me caddy for her at the prestigious Cornwall Golf Club.

I had to hitchhike to the club because I didn't own a bike or have money for the bus. I finally got to the club on the outskirts of town and quickly eliminated any chance of a return to the caddy job. I couldn't refrain from joking, especially when Miss Carothers was lining up a putt. By the end of the day, she abandoned any idea that she could convert me into an angel. However, I still appreciate her interest in me when most others didn't.

## DAVE HICKEY

Dave Hickey was a short, powerful man who taught at Central Public in my era. My antics often irritated him, and he decided to challenge my manhood one day. Hickey told me I probably didn't have the guts to dress up as a girl during the school's annual winter carnival. Soooo, not to be the type of person who would overlook or run from a challenge, I decided to call his bluff and dressed as a girl with my face covered with a mask.

The kids knew it was a male behind the costume due to my hockey skates, but my identity remained a mystery until I removed my mask. Everyone was shocked that the so-called tough guy was playing this role. I proceeded to circle the rink to the cheers of the other students, and a lot of the teachers waved their approval. Finally, I gave a special salute to Mr. Hickey on the way past the podium.

## BOB "TWITCH" TAYLOR

One of the good guy teachers was big Bob "Twitch" Taylor. He had an easy-going manner and had been a basketball star at a university in the States. Many decades later, at a party that the late Big Mike Heenan held at the Navy Club in Cornwall, Bob told everyone about a confrontation with me during grade six. His story was that I was acting like a jerk, and he had to grab me by the shoulders and lift me off the ice as I refused to leave. Taylor had everyone in stitches at the party, telling the tale, then raised his pant leg to show a scar he got when I kicked him with my skate.

I profusely apologized for the incident, and he, of course, being the type of man he was, sat there and almost fell out of the chair laughing along with the rest of us. It was always a delight to see Bob at these events. Unfortunately, Bob passed away several years ago. He was a good guy.

## THE PRINCIPALS

My two principals at Central Public were Mr. Fred MacMillan and Arthur Youngs. MacMillan, a short, stocky man, was quite nice despite my constant behavior problems. So, I felt positive towards that man.

Youngs was another matter altogether. Admittedly I was a thorn in his side and was down at his office regularly. At times I pushed him beyond his control point. In those cases, he would inform me he was going to strap me four times, and I should stretch my hand out. The blows hurt, but I refused to indicate they did.

He would always ask me, "How does that feel?" Of course, being a smart ass, I would answer, "Not too bad." My continued defiance would anger Youngs, and he would respond with more strikes. Whomp, whomp, whomp, and again I would refuse to show pain or submission. Finally, he would give up and send me on my way. My hand would ache terribly, but I had a reputation that I had to maintain, so I would smile as I walked out of the office. I immediately headed to the water fountain and ran the cold water on my hands to ease the pain.

My classmates would always ask me, "How did it go?" and my usual answer was, "No big deal," and then I'd walk away with a smile. But, of course, today, such behavior by a principal would result in dismissal or criminal charges of child abuse: strapping, violent shaking and verbal abuse were considered acceptable in that era; however, it was wrong. The focus was on control of the massive number of kids rather than the mental and physical safety of the children.

But before anyone starts shedding tears for poor Brian, please remember that I was a piece of work. Recall, too, that most of the teachers and principals were good people who did not use violence and verbal abuse to control their charges.

## PERSONAL INSIGHTS

It is interesting, looking back, how I responded to my lack of academic and athletic skills. I was bored to death and had little interest in learning anything about anything. I would leave school at the end of the day and place my books on a shelf near the school stairs. They would be waiting for me the next day.

My mother would always ask me about my homework, and I would lie and tell her I always did it at school. I don't recall bringing home any books the entire time I went to school. I learned to attract attention by acting like a clown, which drove the teachers nuts. Often, I would respond to perceived insults by punching someone's lights out. I was always on edge and took immediate action against anyone who challenged me, whether the threat was real or imagined.

## THE ROYAL CANADIAN SEA CADETS

A friend of mine mentioned that I should get involved with one of the local youth organizations to help me from being so aggressive. So I decided to look into his suggestion.

The Royal Canadian Sea Cadets are a youth organization funded by Canada's Department of National Defense, the Navy League of Canada, and local fundraising. The program's goals include helping Canadian youth from 12 to 18 transition to adulthood. The Sea Cadets develop self-awareness and actively contribute to society. They learn about teamwork, problem-solving, and effective communication, all through the lens of a maritime focus. (I stole that explanation from the Navy League website.)

I loved the group dynamics, the uniforms, and the fact I finally got to be involved in my lifetime love of music. Unfortunately, there was no money for piano lessons and the like, but with the Sea Cadets, there were all kinds of instruments, and I learned to play them all. We would spend countless hours practicing and listening to radio programs and records that featured military bands.

Most of our activities took place at the old St. Columban's church hall, located on the west side of Pitt, north of Fourth Street. Mr. Percy Smith was in charge and did a fabulous job. We were required to do fundraising by selling lottery tickets all over the area. One mythical story was that there was never a winner from these draws. But, interestingly, some claim part of the cash contributed to the purchase of a toilet for one of the organizers, who was relatively poor.

We had a tremendous band that included such great guys as Eddie Upson, Gib McIntee, Larry Gabri, Larry Quattrocchi, Ronnie Price, Billy Philips, and many other terrific people. I'd play the drums, the glockenspiel, the trumpet, and other instruments. I enjoyed the challenge.

We were proud of how we looked in our sparkling blue and white uniforms and loved the discipline and recognition from appearing around the area. I was part of something bigger than myself. I loved it!

## HIGH SCHOOL DISASTER

Unlike the Sea Cadets, high school (CCVS) was a disaster. I was a fish out of water. My academic skills were minimal, my social skills were nonexistent, my clothes were shabby, and aside from hockey, I only participated in a few sports. But, again, I could do the work, but I chose not to. So, as usual, I reacted by playing the clown and taking offense at any insult, real or imagined. It was all downhill from there.

At first, they placed me in a general grade nine class. I had the brains but not the ambition or inclination to become a prize-winning scholar because I was bored to death. Nothing seemed to excite me. Finally, the teacher kicked me out of the sheet metal for taking large pieces of metal and running them through the cutting machine to see how many little bits I could cut up each class. I did the same thing in the woodworking. During art class I painted my desk a fluorescent orange and carved my name on the top, so everyone knew which desk was mine.

The school decided the Occupations area would better suit me. I didn't feel that being moved was fair, but it was probably a unanimous decision.

This section was a notorious two-year course for those deemed incapable of much academic success. The idea was for the students to gain enough writing and reading skills to get by in society. It was a comfortable situation for some students if they didn't hear the occasional derogatory remarks such as "Class for the retarded." There is no question that students in "Occupation" were "labeled" negatively. I hated it and acted out.

## LOVER BOY? NOT!

At this point, I must add that I was not a lady's man. Unsurprisingly, no attractive female was keen on the skinny, poorly dressed kid from the Occupation class, and to tell the truth; I wasn't interested anyway.

That, however, did not mean that I didn't find myself attracted, from afar, to a few beautiful young ladies. Dorothy Katz and Sheila MacDougal still come to mind after all these decades. Sadly, I learned that Dorothy passed away a few years ago.

## MOVING ON

After playing around for two years at CCVS, I was anxious to move on to new adventures and see the world. The local mill jobs were not for me. I had bigger plans.

# CHAPTER TWO

## SIGNING UP WITH UNCLE SAM

### THE REVELATION

It was a Sunday afternoon, and I walked up Pitt Street, turned west on Second Street, and almost ran over three men dressed in military uniforms coming around the corner. I excused myself, took stock of the moment, and realized they were soldiers from the United States Army. I turned around, followed them toward the New York Café, and saddled into a booth directly across from where they had been seated. Being very curious about the design and style of their uniforms and listening to the sound of their southern chatter, I was intrigued.

I watched their every move and listened to every word like a 007 James Bond-trained spy trying my best not to be detected and told to mind my own business. They had various badges designating the branch of service they represented, medals hanging smartly on their chest, and a bearing about them that projected honor, courage, and commitment.

They finished their meal and exited the restaurant. I left right behind them, and I had this overwhelming feeling like the tail end of a Tsunami wave hit me and filled my mind with thoughts of uniformed men fighting our enemies and saving the world. I had finally found the direction I wanted to go with my life; I would join the military.

My first thoughts were to join the Canadian Army and possibly sign up with the Canadian Black Watch, which had a prestigious and highly honorable reputation. The Black Watch's name came from the dark color of the tartan in their uniforms and the original role of the Regiment to "watch" over the highlands. The Black Watch is an infantry battalion of the Royal Regiment of Scotland, and their motto is "Nemo me Impune Lecessit" (Latin) which means "No One Provokes Me with Impunity." They were the oldest highland Regiment in Canada.

I researched the Black Watch and was highly impressed with its accomplishments. Still, the Canadian Army wasn't moving its troops around the world like the United States was, and I wanted to see the world. Consequently, I crossed the border to Massena to see what the American Army had to offer.

## THE BIG DECISION

The next day I took a taxi and headed over the border to the Army recruiting office on Main Street in Massena. I had already researched the Army brochures and had a good idea of what I wanted to do if they accepted me. The recruiter was very receptive to anyone interested in voluntarily signing up for service. But, unfortunately, in this era, the draft swept up eligible young American men, and many were very resentful. So my visit was a nice change for the recruiter.

## DRAFT DODGERS

The recruiter mentioned that it was a little odd that a Canadian would want to join the American Army when so many American Men were trying to escape to Canada to avoid the draft. Because they were not formally classified as refugees but admitted as immigrants, there is no official number of how many draft evaders and deserters entered Canada during the Vietnam War. One informed estimate placed their number between 30,000 and 40,000.

## PAPERWORK

The recruiter handed me the required test, and I went through the pages carefully, answering the questions quickly, then handed it in and nervously awaited the results. It wasn't long before the recruiter gave me the welcome news that I had a great score and was eligible to enlist. I was delighted! We went over the following required steps, and then I proudly exited the office with my papers in hand and took a cab back to Cornwall. What a day!

It took approximately eight months for the American Consulate in Montreal to process the necessary paperwork and for me to obtain a Canadian passport. Once I completed these steps, I raced back to Massena, where the recruiter told me everything was in order, and I was ready to be a soldier. My smart-ass reply was, "Let's get it on! I will be here on Monday and on time and ready to go."

## TELLING MOM

I now had the unpleasant task of telling my mother that I had joined the United States Army and I was reporting in on Monday. To say that the announcement didn't go over very well would be a monumental understatement. Mom was not happy, but she knew that my life in Cornwall and a small town just wasn't my cup of tea, and I had a great desire to go on to bigger and better things. Finally, with tears in her eyes, she conceded and wished me well. I put my arms around her and told her I was a big boy now, would be OK, and loved her.

## BASIC TRAINING

At ten o'clock Monday morning, I arrived in Massena as scheduled, the bus left the station around eleven, and a busload of recruits and I were on our way to Syracuse. The 2 1/2 hour trip was somewhat uneventful, but there was a lot of nervous chatter between the recruits, and those drafted had sullen deflated looks.

Our group arrived at the induction center, and the instructors hustled us into a room to receive processing instructions. We quickly felt this was a military atmosphere, so we should pay attention and get to business. As expected, the staff administered additional testing, including a medical inspection. Then the army personnel told us we could go downtown Syracuse and enjoy our last night of civilian life. Not surprisingly, however, we had to report back by midnight and be ready to be sworn in the following day.

# THE LAST DANCE

The bus load found its way to the entertainment section of town, and we began to see how fast we could get "Stuck in Stupid." It didn't take too long. The drinks were flying across the bar at the speed of light. The ear-piercing music was so loud that we had to yell at the person beside us.

I remember the dance floor pulsating so much it felt like a herd of elephants had just jumped off Noah's Ark. I got tired and wanted to sit down, and the only empty chair I found was at a two-person table with a black guy sitting by himself. I asked if the chair was open, and he waved and invited me to sit and enjoy the show.

My new friend and I immediately started what we thought was an exciting dialogue of alcohol-induced nonsense about worldly matters. Of course, none of the conversations made much sense, but we were having fun. Then he pointed out the guy at the next table, whom he identified as some big shot who wasn't doing anything to help the black people in the country. I listened a little more and finally heard enough. So I leaned over and said that I agreed with his synopsis, and I would go over to the guy's table and explain what he was doing wrong. This decision was another start of my Stuck in Stupid mode.

On my way and in my drunken stupor, I accidentally bumped into an adjacent table. I sent the beer bottles crashing to the floor and had to apologize profusely and pay for another round of suds. I continued to the big shot's table to give him a dressing down. The first thing out of my mouth was, "Just who the hell do you think you are by not treating black people with respect?" He sat there with a blank look on his face and didn't know what I was talking about. So, I went on and on with nostrils flaring and my mouth going as fast as a machine gun with my arms flailing away like I was getting ready to fly over the bar. The conversation ended abruptly when two big monster bouncers lifted me off the floor, deposited me outside the front door, and told me to go home. Being young and Stuck in Stupid, I concluded they were right.

I was trying to hail a cab when another guy approached me and asked if I knew the guy I was yelling at. I muttered, "No." Then he told me it was Daniel Patrick Moynihan, an American politician, diplomat, sociologist, and later a powerful Senator for the State of New York. The guy told me I was lucky I didn't get shot. It would have been nice if someone had mentioned that a little sooner and before I got to the table. I had just moved to the States, and every day was a new experience. Nevertheless, I learned a valuable lesson, don't let your ass overload your mouth.

# THE OATH

We were ready to pledge our allegiance the following day despite being hung over. What follows is the oath I took:

"I, Brian Rouleau, do solemnly swear (or affirm) that I will support and defend the Constitution of the United States against all enemies, foreign and domestic; That I will bear true faith and allegiance to the same; and I will obey the order of the President of the United States and the order of the officers appointed over me, according to regulations and the Uniform Code of Military Justice. So help me, God." We all gave a resounding shout-out and a hurrah; we were officially in the Army.

We were lined up and called to order by one of the drill sergeants and individually called to the front of the formation and handed our paperwork with the location of our new assignments and the post we would be going to next. I was now a part of the massive, powerful U.S. Army, and adventure beckoned me. It was an exciting time! I was heading to Fort Dix, New Jersey.

# WELCOME TO FORT DIX

The U.S. Army established Fort Dix on July 16, 1917, as Camp Dix, named in honor of Major General John Adams Dix, a veteran of the War of 1812 and the American Civil War. Camp Dix was home to the 153rd Depot Brigade. Its role was to receive recruits and draftees, organize them, and provide uniforms, equipment, and initial military training. Depot brigades also received soldiers returning home and carried out their discharges. Fort Dix ended its active Army training mission in 1991 due to Base Realignment and Closure Commission recommendations. Presently, it serves as a joint training site.

The Army bussed us to the vast basic training center at Fort Dix, just outside Trenton, New Jersey. We clamored off the bus and milled around a podium behind which stood a drill sergeant. He gave us a perfunctory welcome and began calling out our names and barracks assignments. I heard "Rolo? Rulolo? Ruminolo? And similar sounds. When no one replied to these names, it dawned on me that he might be indicating yours truly. So, in all innocence, I called out, "Would that be Rouleau?" He unleashed a stream of curses and insults, ending with, "Anyone with a last name starting with "R" is who I am talking about." When I announce anybody's name that starts with an "R," I expect to see your sorry ass double-timing up to this podium. Do you understand that soldier? Yes, drill sergeant. Now drop and give me 20 pushups and count them off loud. Do you understand that soldier? Yes, drill sergeant.

Suitably humiliated, I immediately performed the pushups as quickly and proficiently as possible. At the same time, about 50 other inductees stood there with smiles from one side of their faces to the other. On the first day on the base, I was already a known entity. I immediately tried to maintain a look of anonymity, bowing my head and averting my eyes, hoping to disappear in the lineup of soldiers while feeling like I was dancing on a razor blade. After my grand slam push up introduction to the rest of the men, they instructed us to report to a specific barracks and assigned a bed and locker. It was all part of the program to get us acclimatized with the ways of the Army, and I got the message real quick.

For those of you who have seen the movie "Full Metal Jacket," Directed and produced by Stanley Kubrick, you may remember Gunnery Sergeant Hartman, a harsh, foul-mouthed, and ruthless Senior Drill Instructor played by R. Lee Ermey. He drove Private Pile, played by Vincent D'Onofrio, to suicide. The instruction tactics used in the movie were quite like those used in the 1960s. But, of course, today, those methods would not be permitted. However, it was a time when you had to be able to adjust to the rigorous and sometimes downright nasty things that drill sergeants were allowed. And this was a great reason to keep a low profile during basic training.

As I entered Fort Dix, I faced ten weeks of basic training. The first order of business was paying for a "buzz" cut. Then it was off to get outfitted with a uniform, boots, towels, a comb, a toothbrush, a shaving kit, and assorted other items. The soldiers dispensing the uniform had little patience for anyone complaining their pants didn't fit well! Next, we were required to store away all our civilian clothes, and then we went off for a series of shots to protect us against various diseases. Then it was test time. The Armed Forces Qualifications Test was how the Army tried to figure out in what cog they should place you in their vast machine. The Military Occupational Specialties (MOS) listed hundreds of job classifications from which a recruit could choose one.

Revile was 5 a.m., and whether you were ready or not, the show was about to begin. First, the instructors would enter the barracks and nudge the men sleeping on their cots. By the time they reached the end of the line, they were screaming and throwing the poor souls out of their beds. Next, we had to shower, shave, and dress before 5:30 a.m. Then, we lined up in parade formation for our first inspection of the day. It didn't matter if it was raining, snowing, or a tornado was coming through; you better be out there on time, standing tall and paying attention to your drill instructor.

When we left our barracks, a drill instructor would enter and give a thorough inspection. The barracks with the highest marks would receive "benefits," whereas the losing groups would be ridiculed mercilessly for not living up to expectations. It was all a strategy to create competitiveness, team unity, and high expectations.

## A SECTION EIGHT

Our barracks had a latrine and rows of bunk beds. The food was good, and I liked the training and found much of it interesting. But on the other hand, many drafted kids used every opportunity to resist and complain. They were looking for any chance for the military to reject them. For example, we had one drafted guy from Philadelphia who came up with the idea to lie on the floor and scream and kick while banging his head against his footlocker.

One night we came in after a long-forced march, and he began to yell and bang his head against his footlocker. Being a smart-ass, I yelled out, "Someone find his keys so he can open up his dam locker" I thought it was hilarious, and so did most of the boys, but the drill instructor couldn't see the humor, and I was once again in the pushup mode for a set of twenty.

He received what is known as a section 8, a category of discharge from the United States military used for a service member judged mentally unfit for service. There wasn't anything wrong with him; he just had a case of, I want to go home to my mommy. On the way out, he looked at me with a big smile and a wink. He had beaten the system.

## EARNING A REPUTATION

The above reminds me of what Andy calls my "Chow Line" story. I saw this big mutt skip into the line in front of me in the chow line. There was no worry that the food would run out, but his move was an affront to my sense of order. I took it personally.

He just walked right up to the line and slid in front of this little guy ahead of me, and I was a little confused, so I asked the little guy what was up and did he know this guy. He told me he didn't, and the mutt was making a habit of doing it every day, especially with the smaller recruits. Consequently, I went up to the guy and said, "The line starts behind me, and I would appreciate it if you would be so kind as to go to the back of the line where you belong." Not surprisingly, he took exception to my interference and informed me that he was a badass street gang member from New York City, and I needed to get out of his face before he kicked my ass all over the drill field.

My immediate response was casual: "REALLY? I don't care if you're J. Edgar Hoover in a blue sequin nightgown, and you can beat you won't be kicking my ass anywhere. It was show time, and the bully proceeded to get into a boxer's stance. When I walked away, he was lying out cold on the floor. I proceeded up the chow line accompanied by pats on the back and the "nice job" smiles from the other guys. I had established myself as someone who would not tolerate bully bullshit from anyone.

## BASIC TRAINING

We had all signed up to be a part of the United States Army, and we had, by oath, dedicated ourselves to becoming Army strong. Being a soldier in the U.S. Armed Forces is one of the noblest acts of service, and it would shape my mind, body, and spirit for the rest of my life.

Army Basic Combat Training, aka Army boot camp, is where you build the foundation for your Army career. Recruits learn skills such as marching, repelling, handling weapons, proper dress, and grooming standards, as well as the real-world meanings of discipline, teamwork, and the Army's core values. Basic Training is physically and mentally demanding, and the weak at heart need not apply. The boot camp training cycle is about ten weeks and divided into three phases: Red, White, and Blue.

## RED PHASE

Weeks one through three are the adaptation phase, where we learned the fundamentals, traditions, and ethics of being a soldier. Among other things, the drill instructors taught us how to conduct ourselves and address leadership properly. A requirement was to memorize the Warrior's Ethos and the Soldier's Creed. In addition, we received a briefing on basic first aid and sexual harassment and sexual assault awareness and prevention programs.

This Red phase included intense physical training and road and formation marches. In addition, the drill sergeants made us take the Army Combat Fitness Test, which challenged us on a strength deadlift, standing power throw, hand-release pushups, a sprint/drag/carry, leg tuck, and a 2-mile run. An introduction to Chemical, Radioactive, Biological, and Nuclear (CERN) readiness also occurred during this phase.

## WHITE PHASE

Weeks Four and Five

We had the basics; it was time to dig even deeper. During these weeks, the focus was on self-discipline, teamwork, combat skills, night training, hand-to-hand combat, weapons training, and physical fitness. Learning how to repel down a 50-foot Warrior Tower was a thrill.

## BLUE PHASE

In the final phase of basic combat training, we built on everything we learned. These weeks served as our final transformation from a civilian into a soldier. Below are some of the skills we worked on:

- Advanced marksmanship.
- Maneuvering techniques.
- Team targeting. (Making sure we didn't shoot each other.)
- Convoy operations.
- Identifying and disabling improvised explosive devices.
- Using advanced weapons like machine guns.
- Using live grenades.
- The multiple-day land navigation course tested our fitness and soldier skills.

Week 10 Graduation

After all the blood, sweat, and tears, basic training had paid off. Now you're ready for the 10th and final week, the graduation ceremony. The event lasted about thirty minutes with lots of marching in formation accompanied by a big Army band. Our superiors expressed their congratulations which made us very proud. We were now bonafide soldiers.

## A BREAK

After ten weeks of intense basic training, the Army gave us a short break. I didn't want to travel home, for my buzz cut made me look like one of those homeless guys who received a free haircut from the Salvation Army. My buddies would have teased me mercilessly. So instead, I accepted an invitation from my Army buddy Eddie to travel to his home in Boston. This trip was an eye-opener!

The first night Eddie's friend named Sal drove us around with another guy. At a stop light, a vehicle pulled up beside us, and its occupants began staring at us. Suddenly they pulled out guns and started blasting away! Sal and his friend returned fire while Eddie and I tried to make ourselves invisible in the back seat. It was incredible!

We raced down the road, and Sal pinned the other car against a guardrail and kept it there for what seemed like a mile. Sparks were flying, metal was grinding, and tires were squealing. It was like a Bonnie and Clyde scene from the old movies. I was stunned! Finally, the other vehicle managed to escape down an exit ramp, and it was over. Sal and his buddy were whooping and hollering like they'd won the Superbowl. Eddie was laughing and said, "Welcome to Boston!" Wow! I found out the next day that Eddie had problems with the Winter Hill Gang led by the infamous Whitely Bulger. They dominated the predominantly Irish mob in Boston with the help of a corrupt FBI Agent.

Note:
I was told through the grapevine a few years after my time in Boston that Sal went for a ride and never returned. That wasn't too surprising to me.

This wild event was my introduction to the big city; riding with this bunch was a fantastic feeling, but I knew it wasn't a place I wanted to stay very long. But Eddy's parents were lovely, and I enjoyed their company, and their hospitality was excellent.

Eddie claimed to have played drums in a band that backed up the famous Righteous Brothers (Bobby Hatfield and Bill Medley), who had some of the best soul songs of the sixties, such as "You've Lost That Loving Feeling," "Unchained Melody," and "Soul & Inspiration." I was also a drummer, and that's how Eddy and I initially got together at Fort Dix. I was always banging the drumsticks at every opportunity I had. One afternoon Eddy was going out and asked me if I wanted to play on his drum set in the basement to go and have fun. I was going to town on the drums pretending to be Gene Krupa or Buddy Rich, considered two of the most influential drummers of all time. Suddenly Eddy's mother appeared to politely tell me she had company and suggested I play cards which were behind a curtain in the next room.

To my shock, there was a tremendous selection of roulette wheels, gambling tables, slot machines, and every type of gambling equipment imaginable. The father was running a mini-casino out of his basement. During that era, he had to pay off the local Mafia representative for the privilege of participating in their monopoly. So, naturally, he had to pay for this right, and few dared to buck the system for fear of a beating or worse. Underboss Jerry Anguilo of the New England Mafia Family dominated gambling in Boston. He was no one to fool with, nor his flunkies.

Over the years, I have learned not to ask questions about things that are none of my business, and this was one of those times. I heard later that Eddy's father was connected to the Boston mob and was one of their bagmen who also cared for many gambling machines. The notorious "Combat Zone," an area of Chinatown filled with strip clubs and peep shows, was part of Eddie's father's route. My adventures in Boston ended too soon, but it was time for me to return to Fort Dix and soldiering.

When I arrived back in For Dix, the officer told me I would enter Advanced Individual Training (AIT), where I would focus on a specific job (MOS.)

## ADVANCED INDIVIDUAL TRAINING

I was again assigned a company and barrack location, and the learning process began. The AIT provided extensive training in the given job, so you're ready to hit the ground running when the Army deploys you to your new post. Our training got a lot more intense and covered all of the same subjects we learned in basic training, and we gradually became more and more proficient in each category. In addition, we spent a lot of time on weapons training, including how to dismantle and clean our rifles in record time and every aspect of becoming accurate shooters.

## CHANGING RIFLES

We used the M14 rifle, which weighed 9.2 pounds, used 7.62 caliber ammunition, and had an effective range of 500 yards. Then, when I was in Vietnam, the Army introduced the M16, which was about three pounds lighter, more accurate, and with greater range, although it lacked the penetration power of the M14. Sadly, the M16 initially had a problem ejecting its spent shells, and many soldiers ended up in the middle of a battle with a jammed gun. How many died because of this failure is unknown. Finally, the Army discovered its new rifle required much more cleaning and introduced the required training, and the problem disappeared.

## MOCK VILLAGES

While training at Fort Dix, troops learned how to attack a full-scale mock Vietnam village with civilians, chickens, and trash piles. We had to be cautious with the villagers; some were on our side, and others lined up with the Vietcong. You could not tell just by looking!

Training for deployment in Vietnam considered various factors, depending on the specialization of the unit. This specialization work took place in the U.S., at advanced bases in Asia and Vietnam. The specialists also undertook much of the training for the Army of the Republic of Vietnam (ARVN.) During the war, they continually adapted their instructions as they learned lessons the hard way.

## MOVING ON

Toward the end of AIT, I received my Permanent Change of Station orders So, finally, I knew where I was going on my next assignment.

We finished our advanced training, went through the graduation ceremonies, cleared the post, and I prepared to move on to my new home in Fort Bliss, Texas, right beside El Paso, Texas.

## FORT BLISS TEXAS

After completing advanced training, the Army loaded me and others on a bus and shipped us off to El Paso, Texas.

At the time, the 1700 square mile Fort Bliss was the most significant Air Defense Guided Missile Training Center in the free world. Fifteen hundred square miles of restricted air space allowed for safe missile and artillery testing. The portion of the post in El Paso County, Texas, has a current population of approximately 8,591.

I was excited to be entering Fort Bliss for several reasons, one of which was to be in Texas. The whole experience was something to see, with many of the townspeople walking around with their cowboy hats and boots, and the desert area we passed through on the way to the base was something I had never witnessed before.

Nestled among the foothills of the majestic Franklin Mountains in far West Texas, El Paso is a vibrant oasis in the Chihuahuan Desert and provided me with a beautiful experience.

## THE MOTOR POOL FIASCO

My first assignment at Fort Bliss was working in the motor pool as a mechanic repairing heavy-duty army trucks. I don't know who came up with that idea, but it wasn't me.

One incident I recall was driving a huge stick shift truck from one side of the motor pool to another. I put on quite a display grinding the gears constantly with the truck jerking. Finally, the motor pool sergeant ended my and the truck's misery and I never drove that big five-ton again.

On another occasion, a sergeant told me to take one of the missile launchers three blocks down the road. These vehicles hold three missiles and have treads like a tank. It was sweltering in El Paso, and I was Stuck in Stupid. Combine the tracks and the soft asphalt; the result was tread tracks for three blocks! The sergeant asked if I'd like to transfer out of the motor pool, and I couldn't say yes fast enough.

## THE HONOR GUARD

I went through the drills and became a Fort Bliss Honor Guard member, but I was not excited about my new assignment. Having a sergeant yelling at you every time we practiced was getting a lot like basic training, and I had had enough of that nonsense. It was time to try something else.

## DRIVING THE BRASS

Before applying for a job driving, high-ranking officers around, I got a haircut, had my uniform pressed, and my boots shining like diamonds. When I entered the sergeant major's office, I looked pretty good and felt confident.

They interviewed me about my background and my basic training. Then I sat with about ten other guys as they completed their interviews. Finally, the sergeant major came out of his office and announced that I would be the Battalion Commander's driver and work out of Headquarters. The officers fast-tracked my clearance to overhear confidential information from my high-ranking passengers. In addition, the sergeant taught me how to handle official ceremonies involving the Battalion Commander. After that, I knew I would be OK with driving the brass around in a sedan that I kept spotless.

I enjoyed the job, and it constantly got me in the spotlight with the lieutenants and captains who would try to get me to reveal when their next surprise inspection would occur. Of course, I couldn't and wouldn't do that, but they kept asking anyway.

I remember one graduation ceremony scheduled for a Saturday morning. Unfortunately, a few of the boys and I were out on the town Friday night, and we got in early in the morning. I picked up the colonel and drove to the ceremony. So far, so good. I opened the right rear door for the colonel and snapped an impressive salute as he exited the vehicle; then, to my shock, the sedan started rolling down the little hill I parked on! I had forgotten to engage the emergency brake! Luckily I chased down the vehicle, jumped in, and brought it to a halt. What an embarrassment! The sergeant major chewed me out for a half hour, but I kept my job.

It was always interesting driving the big brass around the base and observing the soldiers jumping to attention and saluting the car when they noticed the colonel's emblem or general's stars flapping on the flags attached to the front of the sedan.

On many occasions, the sergeant major ordered me to drive to White Sands Missile Range in New Mexico, about 118 miles from Fort Bliss The colonel and sometimes visiting generals would inspect and observe missile firings. Now that was exciting! What incredible power!

Every time I drove to White Sands and the colonel finished his inspections, he would return to the sedan smelling of alcohol and looking drunk. I finally realized he kept a flask in his uniform pocket and used it regularly. So the troops he was inspecting must have known he was loaded. One night I had to drive him to a prominent military get-together on the Mexican side of the border. He was in dress blues, and his wife wore a beautiful gown. As we returned, he was wiped out, loaded, and hungry. He ordered me to pull into a McDonald's. Can you picture the vehicle with flags flying and emblems glistening at a drive-through? The colonel was not a classy guy.

One afternoon I had the pleasure of driving for Brigadier General Samuel Lyman Atwood Marshall, the Chief U.S. Army combat historian during World War II. Hill authored 30 books about warfare, including "The American Fighting Man in Action" and "Pork Chop Hill" which Hollywood turned into a film of the same name. Pork Chop Hill was a famous battle in the Korean War where a small group of American GIs held off a massive number of Chinese troops. The New York Times said Marshall's battle account was "a distinguished contribution to war literature."

I often had the privilege of driving distinguished generals from other free-world countries in addition to U.S. generals. There were a lot of interesting conversations going on in the back seat, and I was lucky to be able to listen in. This period in the Army was a great experience.

## MOVING ON

One afternoon I was in the office when the sergeant major asked if anyone wanted to go to Vietnam. Stuck in Stupid, I raised my hand. The Army didn't give me any time to change my mind. Two days later, I received my transfer papers and cleared the base in the headquarters jeep that the sergeant major kindly lent me. I was excited about the Vietnam War but also naive, and there were some hard lessons to be learned.

# CHAPTER THREE

# IN COUNTRY

The Vietnam War was between North and South Vietnam, two countries founded by a 1954 peace treaty.

The United States feared communism would spread to South Vietnam and the rest of Asia. So it decided to send money, supplies, and military advisors to help the South Vietnamese fight the communist government.

In 1955, President Eisenhower sent advisors to help develop the Army of South Vietnam. In 1962 President Kennedy moved about 11,000 more military personnel to Vietnam, but the Viet Cong (Vietnamese Communists) continued to make gains. It was time for America to go all in or leave. Many of the hawks in the military and politics were looking for an excuse to broaden America's participation in Vietnam.

On August 2, 1964, North Vietnam torpedo boats attacked the U.S. Maddox, patrolling the Gulf of Tonkin to support a South Vietnam raid on North Vietnam. This short battle inflamed the American military and press. The Navy believed North Vietnam boats launched another attack two days later, but the evidence was not ironclad. Nevertheless, it was enough to get the US Congress to pass the Gulf of Tonkin Resolution, which permitted the President to come to the aid of any Asian country under attack. The US was now all in.

Note:
Later analysis of the evidence of the second attack proved that it never took place. However, the US was looking for an excuse to escalate its participation in South Vietnam, so if it weren't for this incident, it would have been another.

## THE MARINES ARRIVE

On March 8, 1965, 3,500 US Marines stormed ashore near the Da Rang airbase signaling a considerable escalation in the US's participation in the War. Not surprisingly, President Johnson continued to accept the pleas of his military, and the number of American forces in Vietnam continued to grow. I was part of this buildup.

## THE DOMINO THEORY

At the time, the "Domino Theory" was prevalent. Its supporters believed that if Vietnam fell to the communists, other countries, such as Cambodia. Thailand and Laos would surely follow. The US government, having little understanding of Vietnam and its people, had no clue that the rebellion was a nationalistic movement. In hindsight, Ho Chi Minh's and his followers' efforts were no different than the American colonies fighting to be free of the influence of Britain in the American Revolution.

The colonies sought and received the backing of France, just as Ho called upon Russia and China. Fortunately, France did not secretly control the USA after the American Revolution, nor did China and Russia dominate politics in free Vietnam. But unfortunately, we went into Vietnam on mistaken beliefs, and the soldiers and civilians on both sides paid a terrible price for that mistake.

But I knew nothing of the Domino Theory nor the knowledge that time and education would reveal. The Viet Cong were the bad guys we needed to kill. So, my attitude was, "Let's get it done."

## THE CAT ARRIVES

We arrived in Vietnam and deplaned at Cam Ranh Bay on a scorching hot and muggy day with great apprehension. As I exited the plane, I thought about what Walt Disney once said, "The way to get started is to quit talking and begin doing," and that is what we all seemed to be thinking.

By this time, we had gone through all the basic, advanced, and jungle training, and in our minds, we were ready to take on the world and the Viet Cong.

Cam Ranh Bay was an Air Force Base and logistics facility built by the United States. It was the primary military seaport used by the United States to offload supplies and military equipment. The Army, Navy, Marine Corps, and Air Force units had compounds and members at the base.

Within a short time after arrival, we were assigned temporary barracks, briefed, and given additional equipment, followed by our papers for assignment to our permanent base of operations.

The officer told us, "Do not get too chummy with the guy sitting next to you because many of you won't be coming back!" Of course, we all knew that, but it made us realize this was real.

That night we were taken out doing a short recognizance march in anticipation of what it was like to be in Viet Nam and to acclimatize us for what was to come.

As we marched through the mud and ditches, we could hear the sound of gunshots and mortar rounds exploding in the distance. We immediately felt the fun was over, and it was time to think about survival. It sure wasn't like when you watched war movies from the safety of your living room.

## FIFTH BATTALION, 27TH ARTILLERY

The Army assigned me to the Fifth Battalion 27th Artillery. It was composed of approximately 516 men who manned 18 105mm howitzers divided into three batteries. There was also a headquarters unit along with a support group. I was in the latter. We would stay overnight in Cam Ranh Bay and leave in the morning for Tuy Hoa, a base about forty miles south of the port facility. Before we left, Sergeants introduced us to the new M-16 rifle. We liked them immediately, for they were much lighter than the M-14. Each of us carried three magazines for the new toy.

The M 101 A1 105 mm howitzer was twenty feet long, seven feet three inches wide, and five feet eight inches high. The barrel was seven feet seven inches long and could fire a shell a maximum distance of seven miles. Big 5-ton M39 trucks or the smaller two 1/2-ton M35 trucks towed the howitzers and carried supplies.

## 101 AIRBORNE DIVISION

In January 1966, some general placed our unit in the First Brigade of the famed101 Airborne Division. When the Airborne soldiers were heading into combat, the Army would place the artillery where it could provide close support. The mobility of the towed Ml 01 Al batteries was critical in completing this mission. So, naturally, the guns needed ammunition, and the crew required food and water. Among other things, I headed up convoys of trucks to provide these necessities.

## CAUTION

I do not want to give the impression that I am trying to come across as some hero in this book. Therefore, no one should interpret my writing about my Vietnam experiences as an effort to present myself as a unique warrior who glorifies war. On the contrary, the US Army trained me to perform my duties with dignity and honor, which is what I did.

## CONVOYS

I'm sure many of you have heard the song "Convoy," performed by C.W. McCall which became a number-one hit on both the country and pop charts in the US back in the day. It would have been nice to have that song accompany us on our trips through the jungle roads, but it wasn't available, for we didn't have the radios nor the time to listen anyway.

There were no front lines in Vietnam. So, the farmer or shopkeeper by day could very well be the Viet Cong attacker at night. Furthermore, there were no truly safe places in Vietnam as Viet Cong soldiers attacked towns, cities, military bases, and other locations every chance they got. Add to this danger the presence of land mines and snipers along the roads we traveled. It didn't take much to set a truck packed with artillery shells into a raging inferno. Nothing would happen nine times out of ten, but you worried about it each time you left base.

Each soldier in the convoy had an M-16, plus each truck had a grenade launcher and a 60-caliber machine gun. So, we were loaded for bear and full of testosterone.

One night our convoy of about ten trucks was speeding along a road lined with jungle. We heard gunfire, and it was my job to get my jeep out front and warn the others by radio in the event of enemy activity. Suddenly, we came across Korean troops walking along the road. (They were part of the Allied effort.) They waved us on, but we heard more gunfire as we advanced down the road to a clearing. To our shock, two bodies were hanging from a tree branch by the feet. The soldiers were using them for target practice! I couldn't be sure whether these soldiers were Koreans or South Vietnamese because they were in heavy camouflage and about 30 feet away.

Things quickly got worse when what appeared to be the leader of these men took what seemed to be a Samaria-styled sword and slashed the throats of the hanging bodies, and their heads fell to the ground. It wasn't our place to stop and investigate, so we kept rolling down the road. Welcome to Vietnam!

Another time our convoy was roaring along when I saw a young girl or small woman moving towards the road and our trucks. We immediately yelled out warnings to the girl not to come any closer but got no response. She came closer, and suddenly, there was a tremendous explosion.

She had either stepped on a land mind or was carrying explosives. (Suicide bombing was not an unusual tactic used by the Viet Cong.) The blast tore her body into pieces that flew everywhere. It was a heart-wrenching experience, but we could not stop, and even if we could, there was nothing left of her body to be able to help. The men on the convoy took it very hard because they had children of their own. If anyone thinks war is fun, they have never had the experience.

## THE CAT EMERGES

Everyone was required to pull bunker duty when we were in the base camp area so we could go to sleep and presume the VC couldn't get through to our living space and attack us. Each night the Sergeant would assign a man to check on each of the bunkers. We didn't use radios for the sound would expose our location to the nearby VC. On my turn, I would move between the bunkers and use a little clicker I had that sounded like the chirping of a cricket. I would click click on mine, and they would click click click back then I would enter the bunker. We changed the password every night. It was a dangerous job, and the boys started calling me "The Cat" for the quiet way I did it. Later in my life, the nickname stuck.

OH! OH!

On night patrol, there is no talking, and each man must keep continuous eye contact with the soldier in front. One time three of us took a wrong turn in the dark and lost sight of our other men. The man responsible was doing this pantomime expression, trying to apologize for his mistake, but that didn't help a dam thing! Lost in a jungle infested by VC was not the place we wanted to be. We sat down and whispered to each other and decided to backtrack but to be very cautious not to set off any perimeter alarms so we wouldn't get shot by our men. Then, finally, I could see the wires with cans hanging from them that acted as a warning if disturbed. I yelled that we were "Friendly" and requested permission to enter the base.

The sentries allowed us to enter, and we were safe. However, the officer on duty was furious and told us how lucky we were and that he was just about to send out a search party. He warned us this kind of incident better not happen again, and you can be sure it didn't!

## PHAN RANG

As the months passed, our Battalion was moved about 170 km north of Cam Rahn Bay to Phan Rang. We were now part of the vast First Field Force Vietnam Artillery, which contained 13 other units like ours. That was firepower!

## COMBAT STRESS

Combat stress affects men in different ways. LRRP squads, pronounced "Lurps," were special soldiers who conducted reconnaissance by patrolling deep in enemy territory. The life span of a Lurp was much shorter than the average soldier.

One day I noticed a veteran Lurp wandering about our base camp area. He looked haggard and worn out. Soon he started wearing black pajamas like the VC and would walk the perimeter of our camp at night. This practice was hazardous, for our sentries might mistake him for the enemy. Sentries immediately escorted him back to the base camp and brought him to the Commanding Officer's tent. We thought he was trying to get killed to end his mental misery.

Instead, the Army busted him from a sergeant first class to a private, finally sent him back to the States, and gave him a medical discharge to get mental help. It was a sad situation.

Another battle fatigue situation happened when we were in the base camp area. A corporal doing a lot of jungle patrols got out of his bunk one night and started to strap on his combat equipment. We knew he wasn't due for patrol and asked him what he was doing. He just started to mumble and appeared to be glassy-eyed, and he continued putting on his gear.

He walked out of the tent, headed toward the jungle, and opened fire with his M16 firing straight ahead and yelling, "I'm going to kill them all, I'm going to kill them all." No one dared to try to get close to him while he was firing, but as soon as he ran out of ammunition, we all approached, and he fell to his knees, crying.

We tried to comfort him and finally got the poor guy back to the tent. Meanwhile, half the company came rushing over, ready for combat, suspecting an attack on our perimeter. I calmed them down, and we took the distraught soldier to the medical tent. Later the Army sent him back to the States, where he received a medical discharge. Unfortunately, I saw a lot of that type of incident in my three tours in Vietnam.

## ACCIDENTS

Unfortunately, some soldiers in Vietnam died in accidents. The causes ranged from friendly fire deaths to simple road accidents or where someone didn't follow the proper procedures to stay safe. I was present in a horrible accident caused by a soldier who wasn't paying attention. I wish I could forget it.

I approached our tent when I heard a lot of yelling. Upon entering, I saw a group of soldiers trying to talk one of our comrades out of tooling around with the detonator for a claymore mine. It is a directional anti-personnel mine developed for the United States Armed Forces and fires steel balls out to about 110 yards. It is used primarily in ambushes and as an anti-infiltration device against enemy infantry.

The soldier kept telling his friends that the detonator was only dangerous in the mine. He then proceeded to show his ignorance by pressing on the detonator handle. Wrong! Boom! His right hand disappeared in a mist of skin and blood! The poor guy only had two weeks before returning to the States. Unfortunately, such events were not uncommon; soldiers who ignored their training suffered the consequences.

## WAR IS NOT PRETTY

The following Vietnam Casualty List will provide the reader with information on the 58,220 death toll from the Vietnam War. I also draw to your attention that decades after the war, a few veterans died because of their wounds. Therefore, the US Military rightfully placed their names on the Vietnam Memorial Wall.

Accidents
9,107

Homicides
236

Illness
938

Killed in Action
40,934

Suicide
382

# FRAGGING

Fragging was a slang term used to describe US military personnel tossing fragmentation hand grenades, usually into sleeping areas, to murder fellow soldiers. Hated unit leaders, officers, and non-commissioned officers were the prime targets. The number of known and suspected fragging cases in Vietnam from 1969 to 1972 totaled nearly 900, with 99 deaths and many injuries. Sometimes the offender tried to make it appear the explosion was accidental or caused by the enemy. The term fragging now encompasses any deliberate killing of military colleagues. However, to protect the families, the US Military did not officially report the actual cause of death of such incidents.

Many professional military men believe that an army composed entirely of volunteers tends to create higher moral support and discipline. This move to a volunteer Army, combined with stricter screening processes to rule out drug addicts and misfits and greater attention to soldiers' psychological stress, has reduced the number of fragging incidents.

# REST AND RECUPERATION (R&R)

Between my first and second tours of Vietnam, I took time off for rest and recovery and spent some 30 days in Hawaii. I enjoyed the sites and the quiet nights on the beach watching the Hawaiian Luau, but I felt the place needed to be less commercialized, and I quickly got bored. I had been on beaches along the South China Sea that were much better. But we had to set up a perimeter along the area where we were relaxing and have armed guards keep an eye out for the VC. When it was time to return to Vietnam, I was ready.

# BACK TO BUSINESS

One afternoon I was walking next to the first sergeant's tent, and I heard this loud crying. One of our platoon members told the sergeant he didn't want to carry a rifle and wanted the Army to send him home. This soldier was claiming conscientious objector status after being deployed to Vietnam.

A conscientious objector is an "individual who has claimed the right to refuse to perform military service" on the grounds of freedom of thought, conscience, or religion." The problem was that he claimed that status after he arrived in country. So the sergeant restricted him to his tent until the officers could process his claim. Two nights later, when we had a perimeter breach, he was back in the first sergeant's tent begging for a rifle. He wanted to return to normal status once the action started.

I'm sure he had reasons for getting out of there and back to the States, but there wasn't a lot of sympathy for his position from the rest of the men. They considered him a coward. So the Army returned him to the States, and we have yet to hear the final disposition of his case.

# MORE R & R

When my R&R came up between my second and third tours, I chose Japan. I landed at the airport in Tokyo and immediately remembered my home in Cornwall with the neon lights that used to shine brightly on Pitt Street. Those lights and signs couldn't compare with downtown Tokyo's magnificent display and excitement. Traffic was a nightmare, but I was mesmerized by the whole experience, and I was excited to go shopping and, of course, to the restaurants and nightclubs.

I checked into a hotel, cleaned up, and was ready to hit the town and proceed to get blitzed in some bar; it was the Army thing to do. So I hooked up with a couple of the other guys in my unit, and we went to show the Japanese how much "Stuck in Stupid" we could get.

By around three in the morning, the "Stupid" was coming out pretty well, and we headed to one of the local night spots where they had a band. We paid the cover charge and walked in like part of the Wild Bunch, loud and obnoxious. Military men on R&R filled the joint, so we knew we'd blend in with the rest of the drunks.

The band was rocking, playing the hottest sounds we had heard in a long time. The adrenalin was running high when I saw this big conga drum sitting on the side of the stage all by itself, and I figured it was time to get into the act. So I grabbed the conga drum and proceeded to bang away to the band's rhythm when this guy suddenly tapped me on the shoulder and asked, "Are you having fun, Brian?" Without looking around, I thought it was one of the guys I had come in with.

Instead, to my great surprise and pleasure, it was a childhood friend from Cornwall, Kevin (O'Byrne) Hern, who also served in the US Armed Forces in Vietnam. If I recall correctly, the Marines stationed Kevin at Da Nang. So there was a great deal of back-slapping, beer drinking, and talk about living in Cornwall. It was a wonderful time with Kevin, his Marine friends, my Army comrades, and me getting obliterated.

It was early in the morning when we finally managed to stumble out of the club, and we all shook hands, gave each other big hugs, and wished each other luck. I often wondered if they all made it through their tours.

Decades later, I was in Cornwall visiting my family and stopped by to see how my friend Andy was doing. We started to talk about Vietnam, and Kevin's name came up. Andy said he knew how to get in touch with him, and I said let's do it. Andy had previously found Kevin in Oklahoma, so we called him up, talked for about a half hour, and laughed out loud about the nonsense in Tokyo. It was a great conversation, and I felt good knowing Kevin was still among the living when we said our goodbyes.

## THE AUSTRALIAN BRAWL STORY

After I returned from Japan, we all headed for a nearby beer tent to relax. It was wild, with soldiers from America, Australia, Korea, and South Vietnam pounding back the suds. The more we drank, the louder the trash talk became. Soon playful wrestling turned into the real thing.

Amid all this mayhem, an Australian soldier confronted me about my Canadian heritage. He still had his camouflage uniform, and similar paint covered his face from a completed jungle patrol. This guy was in no mood to be friendly. He saddled beside me and shouted in a menacing voice, "I hear you're a Canadian; if that's so, why the hell are you wearing a Yank uniform?"

I had my mind in "Stuck in Stupid," and I retorted, "Why would that be any business of yours?" He responded, "I'm over here for God, Queen, and Country." So being a smart ass, I replied," I'm all for your God, and I'm all for your Country, but I hear the Queen is a real bitch!" So then, this guy comes rushing toward me, looking like a bull, ready to jump the best-looking cow in the yard.

Within seconds everyone in the place was fully engaged in an all-out brawl. The fun wrestling and the shouting turned ugly; beer bottles started to fly, soldiers were throwing chairs in all directions, and we were in a full-scale donnybrook. This craziness went on for an eternity but was probably only about ten minutes. After that, it looked like a Saturday night WWE Wrestling show in Madison Square Gardens.

Suddenly an Australian soldier snapped to attention and began to sing the Australian National Anthem. Then as if the hand of God came thrusting out of the sky, the volume started to settle down, and each soldier from the different countries stood there quietly. It was unbelievable! Imagine over 50 men all liquored up and brawling, stopping to listen to the Australian sing and pay respect to his country. Slowly the rest of the soldiers looking like they had all just returned from an active jungle battle, moved closer to him and joined hands to sing along.

When the Aussi finished, an American started to sing the Star-Spangled Banner, and then it was my turn to sing the Canadian National Anthem. To say the whole thing was like a religious experience would be an understatement. At the end of the singing, there was a great deal of handshaking, back-slapping, and tears. The fight reflected the combat stress we all felt and had nothing to do with malice between the soldiers of various countries. We were all in this together.

The next day as we loaded up heading back to our base camp, we passed the same group of Australians. As we got closer, they stopped, turned toward the road, and gave us a smiling salute which we returned and waved goodbye. Unfortunately, we never saw them again, and I hope they all returned home alive. These comrades in arms will always be in our hearts.

## THE DEAD

My post was beside a helicopter unit that worked around the clock, taking off and landing. Nicknamed the "Huey" after the phonetic sound of its original designation, HU-I "Iroquois," these helicopters were the workhorse of the Army during the Vietnam War. Overall, the US used nearly 12,000 helicopters in Vietnam, with more than 5,000 destroyed. To be a helicopter pilot or crew member was among the most dangerous jobs in the War.

The Huey was spacious enough to transport medical personnel, equipment, and the wounded. The Huey's dramatically reduced the delay between injury and treatment. The Army and the Marines also used them for aerial attacks.

Helicopters arrived daily at the remote corner of Tan Son Nhut airfield carrying the bodies of United States soldiers, sailors, marines, and airmen lives lost in the unwinnable war. Fortunately, the American government decided that their dead would be flown home instead of buried in Vietnam.

The personnel handling the body's identification at the mortuary were concerned with satisfying the next of kin. Therefore, every step was to ensure the proper identification of the body. Where possible, at the collection point, two buddies of the soldier sign papers attesting to his identity. In addition, they made dental and anatomical charts listing all wounds and physical characteristics and compared this information with military records to see whether they matched. The authorities also sent fingerprints to the FBI in Washington. Once the deceased's identity was sure, the military informed the next of kin by telegram.

There were two mortuaries in Vietnam, one at Tan Son Nhut and another at Da Nang. Military Airlift Command transports flew the bodies home. Those going east of the Mississippi arrived at Dover AFB in Delaware, while the remains destined west of the river went to Travis AFB in Northern California.

Working in this line of duty put unimaginable stress on the people who had to process the bodies each day, and one reporter asked an officer if peace would put him out of business? He replied, "God, I hope so! I've been doing this work for 33 years, and people ask if you ever get used to it, and my answer is NO!"

As the war raged on, we started to hear rumors about some American Commanders issuing orders such as "Kill anything that moves." Artillery and bombs blasted vast areas dotted with villages while helicopter gunships strafed the exact locations. Afterward, troops would move in on what the brass called "Search and Destroy" missions.

While the US suffered more than 58,000 dead in the war, an estimated two million Vietnamese civilians died, another 5.3 million were injured, and about 11 million, by US government figures, became refugees in their own country. Today if people remember anything about American atrocities in Vietnam, many recall March 16, 1968, the My Lai massacre, in which US Troops killed more than 500 civilians over four hours, during which they even took time to eat lunch.


## THE MY LAI MASSACRE

Note:
What follows is a summary that barely touches on the facts of this horrendous case.


In March of 1968, Lieutenant William Laws Calley Jr. and his men arrived at the village of My Lai, where they murdered hundreds of older men, women, children, and infants. Calley would later state in court that an air strike killed innocent civilians. But there was no sign of enemy combatants in My Lai when he and his platoon surrounded the village. Initially, the Army covered up the massacre until a brave soldier named Ronald L Ridenhour wrote to the White House, the Pentagon, the State Department, and 24 Congressmen describing the carnage.

In 1970 the Army brought Calley to court to face murder charges. The military panel found him guilty and sentenced him to life in prison. But, in a complicated series of moves and appeals, Calley ended up with a twenty-year sentence, but the authorities released him on parole after doing about three. From beginning to end, the whole affair was a fiasco. Calley and his angry men committed mass murder and shamed the nation. Calley paid the price, but the others did not. Furthermore, those who covered up the carnage suffered no penalties that I am aware of. To Calley's credit, decades later, he apologized for his crimes and asked forgiveness.

## COMMENT

In every war, there are murders by both sides. Seeing a friend killed will sometimes push an ordinary soldier over the edge, and he may respond with revenge and not calculated thought. If a unit lacks discipline, these actions can multiply, as they did a My Lai. Therefore, each command level must maintain their heads and make it clear to the troops that revenge killings are unacceptable and will result in a court martial. Ultimately it is up to each individual to make the correct decision. Multiple courts have dismissed the excuse that a superior ordered the action.

## HEADING HOME

My time "In Country" was also ending, and my commanding officer approached me and asked if I wanted to stay in Vietnam for another tour I had seriously considered the thought of a fourth year, but the captain told me I only had a few months left on my enlistment and I would have to reenlist for an additional three years to be able to extend for another Viet Nam tour. I was a staff sergeant, and with a new enlistment, the Army would have given me a new rank of sergeant first class. I thought about it carefully but decided I had seen enough of Vietnam and decided to go home.

I received my papers to head back States side, and I was happy. Finally, I would return to my hometown and see my family and friends. The day I shipped out, I said my goodbyes to the guys in my platoon. All the pats on the back and the smiles were tremendous but hard to take, for I was going home, but the guys were staying in this hell hole. They all smiled and joked, but I'm sure they were hoping they were getting on the plane with me. We flew out of Cam Rahn Bay to Fort Lewis, Washington, for a few days, then on to our final posting before being discharged from the Army.

# THE REALITY OF RETURNING HOME TO A HOSTILE WELCOME

When the American soldiers returned home from World War 2 in 1945, the population greeted them as heroes. Cities and towns across the country held parades to honor returning veterans and recognize their sacrifices. But our homecoming was very different, for we returned to a society that did not seem to care about us or viewed us with distrust and anger.

Many young men who fought in Vietnam had difficulty readjusting to life in the United States. Some struggled to overcome physical injuries, emotional problems, or drug addictions from their time in Vietnam. Others had trouble feeling accepted by their friends and families. Some returning soldiers blamed their situation on the antiwar movement and developed a deep resentment toward antiwar protesters. But many other veterans began to question the war and their actions in it.

One of the biggest reasons many Vietnam veterans felt anger and resentment toward the antiwar protesters was that they came from different social classes. Most men who served in Vietnam came from poor or working-class backgrounds. In contrast, many antiwar protesters were college students from middle-or upper-class families. Many of the deferments (official postponements of military service) granted to young men to avoid serving in Vietnam favored those who were wealthy and well-educated.

Studies have estimated that as many as 800,000 Vietnam veterans have PTSD (Post Traumatic Stress Disorder.) Probably just as many others had non-diagnosed mild forms of PTSD. To make matters worse, The US government initially denied that some of the veterans' health problems were related to their service in Vietnam.

Many Vietnam veterans also had trouble earning money and supporting themselves upon returning to the United States. As it turned out, about 250,000 Vietnam veterans could not find jobs when their military service ended. Most of these men did not have a college degree. As a result, some desperate veterans turned to crime or drugs to earn money. Twenty-five percent of the American soldiers who saw combat in Vietnam were arrested on criminal charges within ten years of coming home, most for drug-related offenses. Criticism of the US Military for failing to understand potential veteran problems and providing complete mental and physical support is warranted. They should also have had teams dedicated to aiding their men's transfer into civilian jobs.

# FORT CAMPBELL, KENTUCKY

I received my orders at Fort Lewis to report to Fort Campbell, Kentucky, the home of the 101st Airborne, to serve out my remaining time. The Army gave us menial jobs to keep busy, but nothing significant.

# STUCK IN STUPID AGAIN

While stationed in Kentucky, a few of my military friends and I decided to go out on the town and have a few beers. As usual, the few beers turned into quite a few, and on our way back to the base, we decided to stop at a Kentucky Fried Chicken. We were dressed in our army fatigues and were talking a bit loud while we waited for our order when this little guy came running up to us and started to yell, "You're not supposed to be off base in your fatigues, and you need to get out of here and back to the base immediately!" He was in civilian clothes and was hopping around like the song Willie and the Hand Jive by Johnny Otis. (#8 in 1958)

He was screaming that we were drunk as if we needed him to tell us that. Keep in mind that this little punk who wasn't in a military uniform looked like he just got out of Officer Candidate School and was still a rookie in the Army. He started yelling that he was a second lieutenant and that we needed to abide by his orders. That was when "Stuck in Stupid" kicked in. I grabbed him under each arm and sat him on top of the nearest table and told him, "I hope you get to be a captain someday but, in the meantime, get the hell out of our way and go and sit in the children's section and leave us alone before you get your ass kicked."

Of course, this little runt followed us back to the base, took down the military number we all had on our vehicles, and reported me to the captain. The following day I got an ass-chewing from hell. The captain wanted to know why I had assaulted an officer of the United States Army.

I explained that this little guy was not in uniform and did not show me any identification that he was military. So I thought he was just some civilian trying to intimidate real soldiers. I added that we returned from Vietnam a few days ago and were unaware of any restrictions about wearing Army fatigues downtown.

He had already received a copy of my records and said, "It looks like you have a clean record, and you served three tours in Vietnam, and I am going to dismiss this complaint, but it had better not happen again. You have about two weeks until your discharge, so no more nonsense." "Yes, Sir," I said, and he dismissed me from his office. As I left, he mumbled that the Lieutenant was a little jerk anyway. "The Cat" had slipped the noose one more time.

# A CANADIAN IN VIETNAM

Being a Canadian, many asked why a Canadian would join the United States Army and volunteer for duty in Vietnam. At the time, it was the right thing to do.

Canada never officially joined the fight with the US forces in Vietnam. Eventually, it harbored tens of thousands of American draft dodgers and deserters, but much more quietly, a stream of young Canadians was crossing the border in the opposite direction. Some were dual citizens who may have been living or working in the US. Still, many other Canadians volunteered, driven by a conviction to fight communism or a love of adrenalin.

An estimated 42,900 Canadians served in Vietnam from 1959 to 1972. Three thousand eight hundred were wounded, 325 died in action, and seven remain missing. These statistics were confirmed and written into the Congressional Records by Senator Edward Kennedy in 1974 and backed up by the Senate Select Committee on POW-MIA affairs.

The government of Canada has never formally acknowledged the citizens who were killed or declared missing in action in Vietnam. Still, in 1994 the Royal Canadian Legion officially recognized Canadian Vietnam veterans for regular membership.

While in Vietnam, I was not allowed to fly the Canadian flag, but I always had a small one right beside my cot to show the rest of the men that I was a full-blooded Canadian and was proud to be serving with the men and women of the United States Armed Forces.

# IT'S OVER

My two weeks had finally arrived; the officer gave me my discharge papers, and I cleared the post. I was officially out of the Army and a happy civilian. As I was speeding out of the gates of Fort Campbell, the military police at the exit gate were waving their arms for me to slow down. I waved back with my discharge papers, and they laughed and saluted me on the way out of the gate. Civilian life, here I come.

# CHAPTER FOUR

## MY DISCO ERA BEGINS

I arrived in Cornwall and settled in at my mother's house on Seventh Street and immediately called my old friend Byron Gallinger and talked him into busing to New York City to pick up my new vehicle. While in Vietnam, I could obtain a pile of brochures featuring the latest muscle cars, and I wanted to have one ready as soon as I could get to New York. It was a long bus ride, but we finally arrived in the city and found a place to stay overnight. We walked the streets for a short time and were amazed at the amount of traffic and activity that went on 24 hours a day.

The following day, we went to the dealer to pick up my car. It was a beauty, sitting there shimmering in its electric blue paint. I was so excited that I could hardly wait to get behind the wheel and drive that beast, but I knew I was a little rusty from overseas. Byron eased the vehicle out of the dealership, and we took the main highway heading back to Cornwall. Byron looked like a kid in a candy store, trying out all the different buttons and reviving up the engine to see how fast it would go.

Once we were out of the Big Apple, I told Byron I would take over the driving because I wanted to see what this monster could do at high speeds. So as I put the accelerator to the floor, the tires squealed and smoked, and the vehicle took off like a rocket. It was registered to go up to 150 miles per hour and I wanted to see if I could handle it at high speeds. Talk about an adrenaline rush! I didn't want to push it too much, so I cooled it down to about 130 miles an hour, and we both laughed so hard and we're happy; we had made it without killing ourselves. I would max it out later.

I traveled the streets of Cornwall like a mechanical predator, looking for any fool who wanted to try their speed bump cars up against the fastest car in town. Stop streets, and red lights became the call of the wild when hot vehicles would pull up beside me, and I would always hear the other drivers yelling to me, "Hey, ya wanna drag?" "You betcha," I would reply. Then, the light would change, and the tires would grind out the smell of burning rubber; the smoke was thick and heavy, and we would take off like rockets leaving Cape Canaveral to the moon. When I was in my heyday with that car, I left my tire marks on every main intersection in the city. Aside from having the fastest car in the town then, I also had a Kentucky license plate on the back and the confederate flag on the front, something I wouldn't do today. Talk about getting people's attention! "The Cat" was in town, and everyone knew it.

My mother lived on the corner of 7th and Pitt in Cornwall, right across the street from the Firestone tire store, and I had them put on the extra wide tires on my car. When I finally got rid of it, I rotated all the tires twice before buying new ones. So I put on five complete sets of tires in 18,000 miles. The guys at Firestone used to laugh every time I pulled in for new tires. Talk about "Stuck in Stupid!"

Later the same year, a couple of buddies of mine (who chose to be anonymous for this book) and I decided that a night on the town was in order. So we proceeded to travel to Montreal to party. We hit a few local pubs and decided to visit a few more, but we had to travel a few miles to get there. We came out of the bar a little shaky, walked out into a snowy, blistering cold winter night, and proceeded to travel down Saint Catherine Street in the middle of the blizzard.

I was playing with the accelerator and brakes and sliding down the hill when the light changed, I slowed down but couldn't stop the car from going through the intersection. There was no traffic, so we weren't in danger of hitting anyone. Sure enough, I lost control and wiped out a stop (Arret) sign on the corner of Saint Catherine and Atwater. Not seeing any local gendarmes around, bringing the sign back to Cornwall would be a testimonial of what "Stuck in Stupid" means.

So we tried to put it in the car's back seat. Damn! The cops were in the vicinity, and the red lights were shining. Our Christmas special lighting effects came when a half dozen cop cars flew up to the "big" accident and jumped out of their cars like they were converging on Theodore John Kaczynski, also known as the Unabomber. But, hey, boys, it was only a stop sign, and we were salvaging it to bring it into the local police station like good Canadian citizens. One of the constables mumbled, "En Tabarnak do they think we are stupid?" I was tempted to give him a smart-ass answer but thought differently when one of the other cops mentioned taking us downtown to check us out.

It must have been a slow night at the station because the cops told us we would have us join them for a little bit, and away we went. They let me drive my car, and they followed. On the way, the boys and I were working on our alibies. Finally, the gendarmes presented us to the on-duty desk Sergeant, who looked like he had just swallowed a bottle of very sour pickles. He was about as pleasant as finding a cockroach in your underwear.

Another officer walked behind the desk and sarcastically asked about my Kentucky license plate and what we were doing in Montreal. I told him I was from Cornwall and had just returned from Vietnam. That's when he blurted out, "What did you do in Vietnam, peel potatoes over there?" If he had made that statement to see if he could get a rise out of me, he hit the main prize for the lottery! Within seconds I jumped over the counter and proclaimed, "I'll peal your potatoes, punk." I was getting ready to give him a taste of a Kentucky good old boy two step on his head when half the police department came out of the woodwork to stop me.

Fortunately, when all the activity started, a Police Lieutenant came out of his office, calmed the situation down, and asked me to step into his office. I explained my reaction to the comment that I didn't spend three tours overseas to come to Montreal and hear some rookie cop bad-mouth me about it.

The police lieutenant was an ex-military man who had served in the Canadian Army and told me he understood my reactions. Surprisingly he asked me if I was alright to drive back to Cornwall, and I replied positively. He walked us to my car and explained that it would behoove me to go directly to the Ontario border and not do any sightseeing or stops. I said," Thank you," jumped in the car, and headed home.

On the way out of Montreal, the cops who initially pulled us in were on the other side of the street. As we got closer to them, I put the car in neutral, revved up the engine, and waved. Of course, they were not thrilled with my performance and our free pass from the Lieutenant. I made a point to avoid visiting Montreal while still owning the GTX 440 Hemi. This Cat isn't that dumb!

## STRUGGLING

My friend Brian Harrington got me a job at Pebbles Products on Walrich Avenue, which produced whey. My job was to load the big trucks with 50lb bags of the product. I enjoyed hauling the bags daily because it kept me busy and in excellent shape.

One day Art Runions, the plant manager, asked me if I could run one of the big whey machines. Without hesitation, I said, "Hell ya." But I didn't know one end of the machine from the other, but the pay was better. So I figured I could bluff my way through. As we walked up to the giant machine, Art asked me, "Well, what do you think? Do you think you can handle this baby?" "Sure, all I need is a couple of minutes of training, and we're on the way," I replied confidently. Art walked me through the steps; I was now the "Big boys" machine operator.

On the night shift, we rarely had any supervision. We devised a program that when Art left to go home for the night, all the boys on the machines would head to the roof of the building and consume as much beer as was in stock in the beer coolers. From the top, we could see when the dust on the road into the plant was kicking up, it meant Art was on his way in. We would then hurry down the stairs and stand by the hottest part of the machines so we would be sweating when Art walked in. He would always ask, "How's it going?" We would perform like a Broadway production and, with sweat dripping, tell him," It's boiling tonight, but everything is going just fine." When he left to go home, we'd immediately head up the stairs to the roof and continue our elimination of full bottles of beer.

One night we were all on the roof well into our cups when the whistle on my machine started to howl! I rushed down the steps and immediately saw that the pressure was going crazy! I ran to the release valves and hit the stop button. The machine came to a grinding halt, huffing and puffing, but at least I had saved it from blowing up through the roof.

I had to call Art in because all production had ceased. When he arrived, I was busily separating the big pipes because all of the product going through the lines hardened up, and I had to drill out each pipe. It seemed there was a mile of them. Art was not happy! Soon after that incident, I decided to move on and out of the mill business. I never liked it anyway (smile.)

## WORKING RETAIL

So next, I hooked up with a retail company. My job was going around the country to department store chains like Topps, Two Guys, Arlen's, Shoppers World, and Zellers to review the performances of the staff to ensure they were working to the maximum efficiency and preventing shoplifting.

Soon afterward, they transferred me to North Bergen, New Jersey, about 3o minutes from downtown Manhattan New York. I lived on Bergen Avenue and started to hang out at a place called Sammy's. It was a bar where all the local North Bergen cops hung out. Talk about a bunch of party guys! They were in Sammy's before and after their shifts, and in many instances, they were half in the bag. Drinking on the job was the norm for these guys.

I became friends with a few detectives, and they would ask me if I wanted to ride with them almost every weekend. What a routine! They would stop at half the bars in the area, have a drink or two, and then move on to the next one. A lot of the bar people thought I was one of them. If they got a call for anything, I was dropped off at the nearest bar on the way to the problem area and would wait for their return.

## A DROP-IN ON THE MOB

After a long night with the detectives, they asked me if I wanted to stop at a bar I hadn't been to before, and of course, I didn't have a problem with that. So we pulled up, and there were no cars in the parking lot, and the place looked closed. The vehicles were in the very back of the lot, and there were no lights. When we walked in the back door, the joint was jumping! If you have seen the movie "Good Fellows," this was the place. They didn't tell me that the mob ran the site, but there were a lot of hushed-up conversations going on. As we left, I asked the guys who owned the joint, and one replied, "Fuhgeddaboutit!" So I did.

## CASHING OUT ON RETAIL

I worked in the business for a couple of years, but it wasn't stimulating. I was involved in 45 department stores in six states and three provinces in Canada. Living in hotels and motels across the country was getting old fast.

I was transferred to Toronto and was in the process of making some adjustments in a Zeller's store. I wouldn't say I liked the store's general manager's attitude. However, one day two Cornwall buddies were traveling from Windsor through Toronto to Cornwall and decided to stop by the store and see if I had time for lunch. Now that meant having a few drinks with them too. Oh, oh, "Stuck in Stupid."

The boys tried to convince me to return to Cornwall that night. At first, I resisted, then gave in. Finally, being polite, I thought it was only fitting to inform the manager of Zellers about my decision. When I walked into his office, the arrogant little bastard handed me a stack of advertising and told me to take care of it in a demeaning voice. He was always talking down to his staff, and he thought he could get away with that attitude with me. "The Cat" don't play that nonsense, and I immediately set him straight. I handed him my employee badge and the foot-and-a-half stack of advertising. I told him he could stick the advertising up his ass sideways, one sheet at a time. He was stunned! As I walked out of the store, the staff, who needed their jobs and had no other choice but to tolerate this mutt, silently clapped their hands and had big smiles knowing that he had finally met his match.

Now Mr. "Stuck in Stupid" was back in Cornwall with no job, little money, and living at home with my mom. I was hoping something would change quickly, and it did.

## THE LAFAYETTE HOTEL

Located at 33 First Street East, the Lafayette was where the prerequisites for entrance included being drunk, obnoxious, and wanting to fight. Some semblance of control was due to Alex Mombourquette, the waiter/bouncer and all-around peacemaker. Many nights this powerful man would wade into the frays and put dents in the heads of the non-believers. He was a feared man but respected by the local bad boys who would goad each other to see if they could get away with some nonsense. The playing quickly stopped when Alex would bust their asses and throw them out of the building.

## THE AARDVARK

On April 14, 1974, the infamous old country and western Lafayette Hotel was reborn as the Aardvark, a rock 'n roll facility. Peter Gatien, the future New York City Night Club King, spearheaded this modest foray into the entertainment business. Gatien had made a success of his jean store but was anxious for bigger things. So, he sold the Pant Loft to Rick Baird, who grew his empire around that base. Initially, Gatien was a novice in the nightclub but quickly learned the trade.

They painted the blocky two-store building black as well as the interior. A door on the west side led to the Brass Bed Lounge, named because of the brass headboards used in the decor. The entrance to the entertainment area was on the east side. Two steps led to a small foyer, then five more steps up to the main level. Initially, the patrons would have to knock on the entrance, and the doorman would slide a little trap door open to see who it was. It copied the Al Capone-type speakeasy entrances in the 1920s. However, it was something different for Cornwall.

To the immediate right was a large bar. Straight ahead was a medium- sized dance floor with a bar on each side. Disco balls and Christmas tree lights hung from the ceiling. At the north end was the D.J. booth, where Cornwall's all-time wizard DJ Jack Martel spun the most exciting music selections, kept the dance floor pulsating, and jammed with the locals going crazy.

## RUSH

The club opened with an up-and-coming band from Toronto called Rush. In early 1974 they succeeded with their first album but were not yet the supergroup they became. Eventually, the Rock and Roll Hall of Fame inducted the core version of the group. The Aardvark only had to pay the band a few hundred dollars for a six-day run in April of 1974. It was a financial and artistic success. The club brought the band back in June, again to sold-out audiences.

## DISCO!

But live bands were not the answer, so Jack Martel took Peter Gatien and Brock Abraham (brother-in-law to Peter) to a massive nightclub in Montreal, where Peter got a sense of the new disco rage. Gatien quickly shifted from a rock and roll theme to disco music played by a live D.J. It was cheaper and less complicated than dealing with bands and agents, and it was the future. The youth of Cornwall loved it!

## THE CAT AND FRIENDS COME ABOARD

In some manner, Aardvark GM, Bobby Castleman, contacted me to see if I was interested in helping provide additional security for the new club. After some thought and discussion, I agreed to the job. Needing backup, I turned to my buddies, Bob Megenhardt and Brian Liscomb.

Bob was huge, about 6' 6" and 300 pounds. Brian was much smaller but a fearless battler. They had my back 24/7.

In the beginning, scores of fights occurred in the Aardvark every night. The main culprits were the transient employees of the Trans Canada Pipeline, a few wild residents of the Axwesasne Indian reservation, and local ruffians left over from the Lafayette days. From the rowdies' tables, t beer bottles would sail through the air, looking for a landing spot on someone's head. Every night was a challenge!

The drunken wild ones meandered through the club with intimidating scowls, construction boots covered in the mud, and a thirst for manly action.

My main job at the time was to corral the worst of the bunch and explain the rules of the house. But, of course, if they broke the rules, "The Cat" would immediately start rearranging eyebrows and facial features.

## A CLASSIC

I recall many fights involving our doormen, but this one is worth retelling. Our guy had damaged his arm in a dispute and had to wear a cast. One night, I was across the room and heard a commotion. When I arrived in the area, the doorman stood over a bloody patron moaning on the floor. He was a teacher in the French system and had a reputation for being a pedophile.

Whatever he was, my guy had messed him up, and he was angry. So, it was only a short time before the man complained to the police, who questioned the doorman. My buddy insisted that he was standing there, and the victim ran into his arm with the cast. Not surprisingly, that explanation didn't wash, and he found himself before a judge facing charges. I laughed when he stuck to his story before the judge, who didn't believe a word. He issued a fine and a stern warning and sent my guy on his way.

## FRIENDS?

To illustrate the complexities of having friends who sometimes drank too much, let me relate this story. Those two guys who lured me out of Toronto stopped by to see me before the club opened. Unfortunately, I was busy, so I told the doorman to take the boys to the nearby Grand Hotel and buy them a couple of drinks on me.

A few hours later, I briefly left the club to get a change for the evening. When I returned, I found the doorman drunk out of his mind collecting the cover charges at the entrance. He had money sticking out of every pocket and had to lean against the railing to keep from falling. I took the money, reamed him out verbally, and all he could say was, "Sorry, Boss, you are right." Things only got worse.

I entered the office, and one of my "friends" was urinating into the ice-making machine and laughing his ass off. The other idiot sat with broken beer bottles all over from trying to get a case of beer open and dropping it on the cement floor. Knowing how stupid we could all get with a few beers under our belt, I made an obligatory fuss and called them every name in the book. I ordered them out of my office and into the club, where I would join them for a beer. Then, of course, I had to send out for more ice and give the ice machine a thorough clearing. What the hell? Life goes on.

Most nights, the disco was packed, especially on the weekends. We'd open at 8 PM and close at 1 AM. Thankfully we had the world's best waiter, Richard "Bergy" Bergeron. The guy was a magician with a tray laden with drinks held over his head as he maneuvered to the target table. Bergy never slowed down, and he also had a terrific memory and knew what drinks certain people desired without being told. He was a marvel to behold.

Unfortunately, at least every second night, some incidences required my intervention. I always tried to anticipate trouble and would go over to a loud table and calmly attempt to convince the idiots to quiet down. Often that strategy worked, especially if they knew me or my reputation. But some were always brave with alcohol and had to learn the hard way. Clubs can only exist with the presence of security personnel to keep control. I was good at my job.

Some of you may wonder if I ever had legal consequences because of my security work. This story should answer that question. There was a significant altercation in the club that I was attempting to control. Suddenly some fool grabbed me from behind, so instinctively, I threw the offender over my shoulder to the floor Oops! It was a local cop that I knew.

The officer was embarrassed and hostile and challenged me to punch him. He said, "Punch me, you want to punch me, punch me." So I did, I laid him out with one punch, and of course, I was hauled off to the city lock up for the night. The next day I appeared in front of the judge, and he gave me a 10-day holiday in the Water Street jail. I knew all the guards there because they were our customers at the Aardvark, so my stay was pretty decent, and I got out in seven days. The authorities held me in the executive suite upstairs, so I didn't have to mingle with the riff-raff. Nice to have friends in high places.


# MARRIAGE

Ada was a beautiful girl who worked in the club. I was attracted to her and vice versa, so we started a serious relationship which was terrific. Then we both got stupid; we decided to get married. For our honeymoon, we choose to drive to Florida. We were arguing when we hit Long Sault about 9 miles out of town. Hell of a way to start a honeymoon.

On our way to Florida, a funny incident occurred as we traveled through Baltimore. The vehicle behind me started tooting its horn. Irritatingly he kept this up for at least a couple of miles. Traffic was bumper to bumper on a six-lane highway. Finally, I told Ada, "If that jerk toots one more time, I'm stopping the car and finding out what his problem was and putting a stop to it." Once again,

"Stuck in Stupid" overcame common sense. Sure enough, the guy toots again. I squealed to a stop, jumped out of my Caddy, and ran back to the offending car in a rage. Suddenly the window rolled down, and there sits a smiling Bob Megenhardt. He and his wife had traveled to Baltimore, his hometown, to visit family. His wife saw me drive past by fluke, and they followed in pursuit. It's a funny story but indicates how I was always tightly wound.

After a short period, Ada and I divorced, and we were both to blame. I was too busy being "Stuck in Stupid" and wasn't ready for marriage. I hope Ada is happy and has a long and happy life.

## THE DRIFTERS

In my era, the Drifters were superstars. They had many top hits and sold out all over the world. However, there needed to be more clarity about the makeup of the Drifters. The original group in the fifties had great success but got into a financial dispute with the manager who owned the name. There was no negotiation, just "You're fired!" Fortunately, Bill Pinkney went on to many decades of fame playing under the moniker "Bill Pinkney's Original Drifters."

George Treadwell, the manager, reloaded the Drifters by hiring a group called the Five Crowns, featuring such talents as Charlie Thomas, Ben E. King, and Rudy Lewis. These Drifters sang hit after hit. Sadly, Lewis passed away at a very young age in the mid-sixties, and the group replaced him with a talented singer named Rick Sheppard.

Rick was with the Drifters from 1966 until 1970, when a financial dispute with the manager resulted in Sheppard leaving the group. Sheppard bounced around before beginning to perform as "The Drifters featuring Rick Sheppard." Rick continues to do his Drifters review to the present day to great fanfare. He is a super guy.

I convinced owner Peter Gatien to let me book Rick's Drifters at the Aardvark. This package wasn't disco, and the size of our place meant the gate wouldn't be great, but we might break even. Also, the Drifter's famous name might help increase our profile in Cornwall and surrounding New York State. So I set up a radio interview in Massena. New York, which is about fifteen miles over the U.S. border. Over the bridge and on the way there and back, I sang with Rick and the Drifters songs like This Magic Moment, Stand by Me, Under the Boardwalk. I just loved their music. They did two shows which both sold out. The Drifters were terrific! We bumped the cover charge up to five or ten bucks to help pay for the group.

# YEARS LATER

I liked the group so much that I booked them in a club I ran called J.J. Whispers, the biggest club in central Florida, before Disney World opened up Pleasure Island. I also booked them into the Limelight in Atlanta for one of our anniversary parties. After they played their set, I took Rick over to one of our guests for the night, Quincy Jones from "We Are the World," fame. When I introduced Rick to Quincy, Rick was beaming like the North Star and was very excited to be in the same company as Quincy. Someone took pictures, and it was a wonderful experience. Of course, I had to get my mug in the photo, and I would bet that Rick still has that picture prominently displayed at home.

# BOBBY CASSELMAN AND I

Aardvark General Manager Bobby Casselman was the hammer on the job for a long time, and when he stepped into the club to settle the rowdy's down, you can be sure they followed his orders. We often had to put the B & B Express into action.

I remember one night when two brothers were causing trouble in the club, and Bobby was addressing the problem. So I went over, and one of the brothers picked up a door jamb off the floor and hit me on the head. I was strong like a bull and smart like a doorknob in those days. So I immediately took offense to this punk and, between Bobby and myself, took care of business.

The guys ran out of the back of the club, and the cops were out there waiting for them. Consequently, the officers asked us to come to the station and identify them. So we went into the cell area, and I asked the Sergeant on duty where they were. He told me they were the two in the back cell breathing out of their ears.

I had to go to the Cornwall Community Hospital and have my head stitched up. The doctor was preparing me for the stitches and started to give me a needle to ease the pain. Being "Stuck in Stupid," I told him not to worry about needles and start stitching.

Now, this might seem brave, but after the first stitch, I knew that was pretty damn stupid. I didn't want to lose respect, so I sat there nice and quiet. When he finished, I thanked him and left the room with my head throbbing. As the famous Scottish poet Sir Andrew Barton wrote," I am hurt, but I am not slain. I'll lay me down and bleed awhile, and then I'll rise and fight again " That was me in those days.

# MANAGEMENT

When Bobby decided to leave, Peter asked me if I was interested in being General Manager, and of course, I immediately said yes. I recently returned from Vietnam and was still wired for sound. The U.S. Army trained me to go from zero to a hundred in seconds, and I used what I called "The bullshit barometer." I could go along with a little bit of bullshit, but once you hit the right spot, all bets were off. At 6" 1', 225lbs, I wasn't the biggest man in town, but I was the quickest and deadliest. There was never a twitch of a muscle or an eye movement that I would miss when confronted by some punk looking to get dusted.

I know we have all seen the big bouncers in the bar scenes of the movies who have muscles running out of their ears, an I.Q. of four, and a slap jack in their pocket to do more damage to their opponent than they can do with their bare hands.

I was none of the above. I learned my skills at different times and places. Those big, muscled brick heads, the Karate and Judo trained bullies, didn't impress me at all Anyone who must announce that they are a black belt in the martial arts is very likely not a black belt in anything except the art of trying to intimidate their opponent. Their jab you in the chest or grab you by the shirt tactics were immediately met with a flurry of punches designed to bring the bullies to their knees and then to the floor with a resounding thud.

I have my comfort zone. If my opponent stayed out of my comfort zone, I was calm. Enter my comfort zone, and the party is on! When I finished dealing with the pest, I immediately proceeded to eliminate any thoughts of them returning for a second round later. I would eliminate their future challenges by providing them with multiple contusions, abrasions, and a great deal of hurt and pain. In addition, I made a point to ensure that any non-believers in the crowd immediately got the impression that they had better think twice before they challenged "The Cat."

There were nights in the Aardvark that seemed like the Gary Cooper movie High Noon. The word got out around Cornwall that this guy from out of town working at the Aardvark thought he was a badass, and almost every night, some fool wanted to see just how bad I was. At the time, most people didn't know that I was originally from Cornwall, had just recently returned from three years in Vietnam, and was as crazy as a bed bug. I took on all comers, and my reputation grew. It is amazing how the word gets out that there's a new sheriff in town.

## THE OK CORRAL

One night a bunch of guys from Massena, who had been thrown out of the club the week before, returned with reinforcements. One of them banged on the front door of the Aardvark and challenged us to a dance in the parking lot. All the security and management team looked at each other and looked at me, and of course, being "Stuck in Stupid," I yelled out, "Hell yeah!"

Out the door we went, and the dance began. The mutts had come with hockey sticks and baseball bats, and we weren't as prepared; we only had baseball bats. We met the challenge, and the fight became a wild sight of tangled, struggling bodies trying to overcome each other. Guys were lying on the ground moaning, and others were running around like Willie Coyote chasing the Road Runner! There was blood all over the place and a lot of yelling. The brawl lasted for about half an hour before the cops pulled up and started throwing these idiots into their cars and told them to get out of town. They vowed to return, and I had to give them my parting words. I said, "I will see you again," and I did.

## ROUND TWO

A week later, I was alone at the Willow Grove bar in Massena. I'm not sure what ever possessed me to go into enemy territory alone, but it wasn't uncommon in those days. I entered, and within seconds I was recognized by the local boys. They jumped up from their stools and confronted me with the bluster of gamecocks, jumping around with their arms flaying and making challenges to kick my ass all over the dance floor. However, they were smart enough to stay out of my comfort zone.

I decided to leave the club before someone called the Massena Police. I walked outside and started my Cadillac up just as a bunch of them came running out of the club. In those days, I used to rap a silver dog choker chain collar around my right wrist, and I could flick it out as protection if my opponents outnumbered me. Out came the chain. Their response was to yell at me to drop the chain, and then we would see how bad I was.

I continued to goad them into stepping forward. Finally, about eight of them faced me, and undoubtedly one fool would like to make the trip to Disney World that night. I yelled out to the leaders and told them, "You guys aren't going to be playing pigeons on the monument with me, not tonight or any night." I am sure they had difficulty comprehending that statement, but I thought it was very eloquent.

None would venture off the steps. Instead, they kept yelling for me to drop the chain. Now my Mommy always told me not to talk to strangers, and I sure wasn't any dummy to do that, especially when outnumbered eight to one. So I calmly stepped closer and put my business card with Brian Rouleau, General Manager Aardvark 33 First Street East Cornwall, Ontario, Canada, on the steps in front of the howling gang of local toughs. Then, to add insult to injury, I yelled back at the punks and invited them over to Cornwall some night for fun times. Surprisingly, a couple of them showed up at the Aardvark the following week looking for me.

One of our customers came into the club and told me there were a couple of guys at the front of the club sitting in their car with New York plates asking for me. So, being "Stuck in Stupid," I turned to Bergy and told him to watch my back just in case there were more than two.

Out the door, I went, and before they could say anything, I yanked the driver through the car window and proceeded to show him how I did the Tennessee Waltz in Canada. The other guy came running around the car, but I intercepted him with a right hook to the jaw. After that, I started to sing, "Roll me over in the clover, roll me over, lay me down and do it again." As the fight progressed, people from the club came out, stood on the sidewalk, and joined me in the song about hookers, but I thought it was appropriate for the occasion. Go figure.

As the entertainment continued, we moved into the front of the Kastners Men's Store next to the Aardvark and ended in the little foyer of the store. I was getting bored with the activities, so I figured it was time to put the boys to bed. I then threw each of them through Kastners' plate glass windows. It turned out to be a real mess with the broken windows, but as in all good things, the party had to end. I returned to the club with our customers while the Massena boys hurried back to their car and sped towards the border. The cops showed up and called the store owner so he could have plywood put up to secure the place for the night until they could replace the glass in the morning.

The next day I went to Kastners, and Nathan, the owner, said, "Brian, you have to stop using my windows for this type of activity." I offered to pay for them, but insurance covered his cost. Nathan was unhappy with my performance, mainly because it wasn't the first time. I promised him I would go out of my way to make sure his windows didn't get broken again, and I did. As a bit of compensation to Nathan, I bought many clothes and asked my staff to do the same. Nathan was a real gentleman, and his Kastners was/is one of the city's best men's stores.

## DRESSED UP

The Aardvark was a great place and the best show in town for a long time. We had lines standing outside every weekend, and the girls would show up all dressed to the nines, with their makeup and hair done perfectly. The problem was that the boys in Cornwall went to the bars in worn-out blue jeans, t-shirts, old running shoes, and the ever-present baseball cap.

We started a dress code to discourage them from coming in looking rough and tough. We figured they didn't mind fighting and getting dirty in their old clothes but would be reluctant to do so in good duds. So the dress code consisted of no blue jeans, a shirt with a collar, and no hats. We also started an all-new $1.00 cover charge. For icing on the cake, we enforced a rule that if we ejected you from the club, we would not let you return for one year. We were the city's hottest club, and the male patrons quickly realized that we weren't fooling around about running a professional operation with minimal nonsense.

## DISCO HISTORY

The Disco era was born on Valentine's Day, 1970 when David Mancuso opened a club called The Loft in New York City. It faded in 1980. When the Disco movement peaked in 1978-1979, the demographic was predominantly white, heterosexual urban and suburban middle class.

Clubs often held Disco Nights, which served as a way for people to socialize and escape from their everyday lives. The genre is important because it encouraged self-expression through dance while also serving as an outlet for people who felt unheard or oppressed by society.

Early disco dance formed between 1966 and 1974 in the discotheques in Philadelphia (The Philadelphia Sound) and New York City (most notably in the private parties of the famous nightclub The Loft. "Soul Makossa" by Manu Dibango from Cameroon was one of the first songs by an African to gain global popularity. Some believe it was the first disco record.

## MAC'S ROULEAU STORY

Claude MacIntosh, Cornwall's favorite Seaway News columnist and Cornwall City Council member, recalled the following:

It was a balmy spring afternoon - late April 1998 - and despite the beautiful view across the park and St. Lawrence River, I was the lone patron sitting on the Royal Canadian Air Force Wing patio when a rider on a Harley-Davidson pulled into the parking lot.

He propped up his 'hog' and draped his leather jacket over the handlebars. The guy had to be 6-foot-2 and 250 pounds. Minutes later, he emerged from inside the bar area with a large mug of draft beer. "Mind if I sit with you since nobody else is out here?" he suggested. It turned out he was from Quebec and grew up in Valleyfield. "I haven't been here (Cornwall) in years," he said, "The only place I remember is a disco joint downtown. I think it was called the Aardvark or something. A trendy spot with lots of hot ladies." He went on to relate the following story.

Back in the day, he and two buddies decided to ride to Cornwall from Valleyfield to check out the place and its supposedly tough manager. It didn't take long for us to realize this guy they called Brian was 'our' man. So sarcastically, I said to my two buddies, "And they call this guy tough? He doesn't look like much. Maybe we'll try him later.'

The biker continued, "People had packed the place, and a waiter with a big handlebar mustache was working the floor. He would carry a tray of drinks with one hand, lifted over his shoulders, a real pro. But unfortunately, three big guys who looked like young construction workers kept bumping into him, hoping he would spill the drinks. The guy called Brian who saw this and followed the waiter back to the bar. We heard him ask the bartender to fill four glasses with water, and then he followed the waiter, who weaved his way through the crowd. Suddenly it happened! The construction mutts bumped into the waiter, and the drinks went flying. Wham! Bam! This Brian (Rouleau) guy was all over the three troublemakers and threw them out the side door. I turned to my two buddies and said, 'Not tonight, guys.' "

## THOUGHTS ON FIGHTING

I never enjoyed the fight game, but because of the circumstances and the business I was involved in, it seemed the only way to keep the bullies and riff-raff out of the clubs. So I was like a moth attracted to a flame when the action started.

Being challenged regularly made me highly cautious everywhere, I went. I was on the alert in restaurants, bars, or anywhere there was a group of people I didn't know. I sat down with my back against the wall, always anticipating some unexpected stranger jumping into the scene and trying to take me out. My style was never to walk into a place and be loud and boisterous but to mind my business and watch the crowd. This type of activity probably seems strange to many, but, it had a lot to do with my military training and background. In most cases, the loudmouth at the bar is not the one you have to watch; it's the guy sitting by himself and minding his own business that you need to be concerned about if there is any action.

# CHRYSLER

One afternoon I was approached by a guy who had been referred to me by a friend. He owned a country bar in Chrysler, Ontario, and was a Firefighter in Cornwall. We met, and he explained that he was having a lot of trouble with the farm boys, hurting his business. He wanted to know if I was interested in settling them down so he wouldn't have to worry about losing his liquor license. I told him I would work it into my schedule, and I did.

I told this fellow not to mention that he was bringing me in, and I drove out into the country to see what his problems were. I sat there eating a meal when this big-ass farm boy came in and wasn't there five minutes before he was raising hell about his order. He didn't get his beer delivered fast enough, and when it arrived, he poured it on the floor, made a few vile remarks to the waiter, and left without paying. I spoke to the owner and asked him when he wanted me to start. He mentioned that tomorrow was Friday, and the problems always escalated on the weekends. I assured the owner I would return, but I made him promise that he was not allowed to get in the way when the action started.

Friday night, I played the role of a new waiter. Guess who showed up smelling like he had just gotten off the hay wagon? You got it! The big jerk from the day before. I walked over to the table and politely asked him what he would like. He looked up at me and said, "I want my regular," and I smiled and asked, "And what would that be, sir?" He pushed his chair back and loudly yelled, "Where the fuck is the regular waiter?" Still smiling, I looked him in the eye and told him, "I am the new waiter, and if you have any complaints, please direct them to my attention."

He then began to yell at me in a very belligerent and menacing tone. Finally, he yelled out, "Do you know who the fuck I am?" I turned my head slightly, seeing the owner looking over our way, waiting for my reaction. I looked the guy in the eye and leaned over, and whispered in his ear, "I don't give a fuck if you're the Lone Ranger who just got done fucking Tonto. Would you like me to explain that slowly so a dipshit, cow-smelling peckerhead like you would be able to understand what I just told you?" He then jumped out of his chair with malicious intent and was met with a right elbow to his overly large mouth. He fell to the floor, and I immediately proceeded to do the Bristol Stomp on his sprawled-out body. He was still squealing like a fat pig when he hit the dirt in the front of the building. He staggered into his pickup truck, mumbling something about coming back, and he did.

The next day was Saturday, and as sure as the snow falls in the winter, the jerk walked into the restaurant with two of his moron friends. As they walked to an empty table, one of the guys tipped over a chair and started laughing and looking over my way. I assumed the fat mutt had brought his backup boys to teach me a lesson that this was their watering hole, and they would do what they wanted when they wanted without any repercussions from the restaurant's help.

I calmly walked over to the table and told them that we would not serve them because of the problems they had caused over the last few weeks. The three losers stood up and told me it would take more than me to throw them out. That's when I proceeded to do just that. They were big and strong, but I was fast and very agile at the time, and within a couple of minutes, they were all in the front of the building, nursing their bruises and still yapping away.

I went through a lot of that type of nonsense during my time at Chrysler, and gradually the bullies in the neighborhood stopped coming around. The elderly customers that the owner wanted started returning. They said they felt more secure and enjoyed the atmosphere much better without the rowdies.

## BIG BILLY DROPS IN FOR A VISIT

One evening when I was getting ready to close the Chrysler place, my friend Billy Ingram pulled up to say hello. Billy was returning to Cornwall after racing his horse at the Rideau Carleton track. It was frigid, and the blowing snow made visibility almost nonexistent.

Billy came in, dusted the snow off his jacket, and said he would stop for a quick beer and let the weather settle down. Billy had a buddy with him, and I had a couple of leftover customers who were friends of mine, so I shut off the outside lights and turned the inside ones down low since we were supposed to be closed. I didn't want any problem with the OPP.

Everything was going fine for about an hour and a half when Billy jumped up and remembered that he had one of his horses outside standing in the trailer. It was too cold outside for the horse, and Billy asked me what he could do. We were heavy into our cups being "Stuck in Stupid," I yelled, "Bring the dam thing inside." We all started laughing so hard we could hardly talk, but we had to get that horse warmed up quickly. One of the guys opened the front double doors, and we guided the horse by gently lowering its head and ensuring he could fit through the doorway.

We cleared some tables so there would be enough room for the animal to be comfortable. Suddenly, the jukebox started, which startled the horse. The boys were pretty loaded, and one of the guys leaned back in his chair to pull on the light switch, but he hit the fire alarm, which started ringing! The music was blasting; not surprisingly, all this commotion spooked the horse, which pooped all over the dance floor.

I called the fire department to tell them it was a false alarm. Meanwhile, the others were trying to calm the horse down so we could get the animal out of the place before the cops and the fire department pulled up. I tried to get the poop cleaned up but didn't do an outstanding job. Finally, we got the horse into its trailer and pulled it, and the truck to the back of the hotel as the fire department arrived. Despite my explaining that it was a false alarm, they insisted on inspecting the rooms on the second floor to ensure no one was there. After their inspection, one of the firefighters said, "I hate to tell you this, but the place smells like horseshit! It was another night, "Stuck in Stupid." I stuck around the Chrysler operation for a couple more days, but I had finished my assignment, the owner was happy, and it was time to move on.

## HEADING SOUTH

A couple of weeks later, Peter asked me if I was interested in going to his new Limelight Club in Hallandale, Florida. Of course, I was excited by a new adventure, so I quickly cleaned up things in Cornwall and headed south.

# CHAPTER FIVE

## THE LIMELIGHT IN HALLANDALE FLORIDA

By mid-1966, Gatien had outgrown Cornwall and the Aardvark. After combing the real estate market in Florida, he came across a location in Hallandale, Florida, a place called Rum Bottoms that was initially called The Heidelberg, a German Restaurant Entertainment Center.

Rum Bottoms was once one of the best clubs in Florida but fell on bad times and was up for sale.

Located at 10001 North Federal Highway near the world-famous Hollywood Dog track, the original Limelight Discotheque was born with Peter Gatien at the helm.

Hallandale, at the time, had a population of around 28,000. The tourist town snuggled in with Miami about twenty miles south and Fort Lauderdale 10 miles north. Today, the municipality's name is Hallandale Beach indicating its location on the Atlantic Ocean.

Rum Bottoms sat on a lot at 1001 N Federal Highway, near the still famous Gulf Stream Racetrack and Casino. (Owned by the Canadian Stronach Family) Reporters for the Miami Herald interviewed Peter Gatien, who described himself as the new owner.

Gatien declared he would pour an unheard-of $250,000 into a state-of-the-art sound and light system. By all accounts, that aspect of the operation was a spectacular success.

The Hallandale Limelight opened with 40,000 special effects lights revolving in a mirrored ceiling, "After the Limelight, everything is just another disco." "A Glitter Palace" as described in Billboard Magazine.

I had decided to go to Florida because I was eager for a new challenge. They had completed all the renovations before I arrived, and when I first entered the building, I was immediately impressed with the special effects lighting and the tremendous sound system.

I had to find a place to live when I got there, and Peter hooked me up with Steven Moore, one of his men. For the first couple of days, I stayed in the back room of the club on a cot. I didn't have the time to find a place to live, but eventually, Steven helped me find an apartment just up the block from the club.

## THE LIMELIGHT CREW

The employees who worked at the club had to be the best to keep up with the amount of volume the club was doing. If they weren't quick, they were looking for work elsewhere. We had some great employees in the Hallandale club, including Allstars like; Tommy DiNardo, Tommy Buckley, Joe Pisa, Steven Moore, Sal Mangino, and Bobby Lombardi.

Bobby Lombardi was, without a doubt, one of the best D.J.s in America. He was the inventor of the B.P.M. (beats per minute) mixing. The master artistically handled the unbelievable mix of music in coordination with the magnificent 40,000 special effects lighting system.

As things evolved, I began working with Stu Stone, head of security. He was a powerful man who was intimidating in appearance and very much in tune with our serious bad guys from New York, New Jersey, Philadelphia, and of course, the Miami area. Stu was originally from New York and was very much aware of the ways of the streets and the people who control them. On many occasions, Stu saved some of our security people from overstepping their bounds by interfering with the wrong people, their sons, and daughters included. Over the years, I had worked in many of those cities, and I knew many times it was very prudent to walk away. Thankfully, Stu was my best friend, and every night we would stand by the door and talk about solving all the world's problems.

## CONTROLLING THE CROWDS

We opened the doors at 8 PM, and the party continued until 6 AM. As the crowds lined up, Stu and I would handle the door. We'd always dress in a collared shirt, sports jackets, and sharp slacks and shoes because we had to enforce our dress code and look sharp.

In the nightclub business, the entrance is the critical spot to root out trouble before it begins. We had a couple of monster-size guys who also worked the door. One was Fred Ottman, who later became a professional wrestler trained by Rick Flare and performed under the name "Tug Boat." Freddy was 6ft 6in and weighed about 384 pounds; his sidekick was about the same size and weight. They both owned new Corvettes and would travel together; you can imagine the onlookers' reactions when the cars pulled up and these two guys exited their vehicles.

We had other security men throughout the club; they were all big muscle builders and looked mean. At 6ft 1in, I was the smallest one on the crew. I looked like a little guy every time I stood beside them. I got the impression that they figured, what the hell is this guy going to do if we have trouble in the club?

## EARNING A REPUTATION

Working the door one night with the boys, this big, muscled guy came up and sarcastically asked loudly. "How much does it cost to get into this joint?" I stepped forward and told him the cover charge, and he gave me the "bad boy eye" and proceeded to throw the cover charge on the counter. Being the type of person I was, I gave him back his change the same way he had given it to me. He looked at me and remarked, "What are you, some sort of smart ass," I replied with my smart-ass attitude and told him, "I don't have to be much of a smart ass to deal with a jerk off like you!" He immediately started to take his jacket off and proceeded to step forward while telling me that he would kick my ass all over the lobby. Now anyone who has ever worked in the nightclub business will tell you it's not too bright telling someone you're going to kick someone's ass while you're taking your jacket off. Immediately my Stuck in Stupid attitude kicked in, and I turned this mutt every way but loose. To make a long story short, they took him away in an ambulance, and that was the last time I heard any rumbles about me being able to carry the load In the event of trouble. Stu said, "I guess Peter was right about you."

# CELEBRITIES ABOUND

The Limelight was an exciting place to be in the 70s. When the Village People churned out "Macho Macho Man," "In the Navy," and "Y.M.C.A.," the crowd was on their feet and singing along with arms waving.

One time the always-exciting Grace Jones walked on top of one of the bars and kicked drinks all over the customers while singing and almost caused a riot. The crowd went wild.

In 1977 Grace secured her first record deal resulting in a string of dance-club hits, including "I Need a Man" and her acclaimed reinvention of Edith Piaf's classic "La Vie En Rose." She is still performing.

Not to be missed were the "Tramps" singing "Disco Inferno" from the movie Saturday Night Fever." They were an American disco and soul group based in Philadelphia and were one of the first disco bands. The band's first significant success was their 1972 cover version of "Zing! Went the Strings of My Heart." In 1976 they had a big hit with "That's Where the Happy People Go."

John Travolta and the Saturday Night Fever movie was big at the time. So one night, I was in front of the club with Denny Terrio, one of the disco-era pioneers and the coach and choreographer who taught John Travolta how to dance. He showed me some of his moves, and the crowd outside loved it and cheered him on.

The club regularly featured the best groups on the Billboard Charts and lines formed around the building. Some groups I recall are; Gary Lewis and the Playboys, Celi Bee, Sister Sledge, Peaches and Herb, Natale Cole, Evelyn "Champagne" King, and many other great performers. The Limelight was the ultimate destination for disco in Florida and quickly became the model for clubs worldwide.

# A JERRY LEWIS STORY

In 1979 comedian and movie star Jerry Lewis was attempting a comeback. He had fallen into the hell of prescription drug abuse brought on by the pain of an injury. His idea was to write and star in a movie about a bumbling character who lost his job as a clown in the circus and was looking for work.

Lewis and his crew filmed all over Florida before arriving at the Limelight, where the fictional character would attempt to be a D.J. The club permitted the producers to build a much larger D.J. booth to meet the filming requirement. Jerry fumbled around, dropping discs and doing his regular slapstick comedy style.

One afternoon a couple of guys came into the club and asked if anyone was interested in being in the movie. I thought they were just kidding, but I volunteered, and they gave me an address and instructions on how to get to West Palm Beach, where they were shooting.

The producers hired me to work in the fictional nightclub where Jerry was a bartender in a strip club with one of our men as the second bartender. The scene started with the girls dancing on the bar, and Jerry was spilling things all over in his usual comedy style. Suddenly he grabbed one of the girls around the legs, so the other bartender picked him up and set him on top of the bar. I walked in with my white suit on; I picked Jerry up off the bar and carried him out the door.

Because Jerry was a perfectionist, they filmed the scene at least 15 times, and I sat around almost the whole day because, after each take, they had to clean up the mess that Jerry made behind the bar. But it was an exciting day at the movies, and meeting and talking to Jerry was pay enough for me. And that, ladies and gentlemen, was my introduction to Hollywood. And my only introduction to Hollywood. I made fifty bucks for the day's work and got a glimpse of behind-the-scenes in making a movie.

The producer ran out of money during the filming and the company suspended production. Then Lewis had to declare personal bankruptcy. Things got back on track when a new producer came in with a $1 million cash infusion.

At first, Lewis needed help getting any company to put the film out in the United States. However, eventually, the product grossed $49 million worldwide. Despite this financial success, critics hammered the film, with some calling it the worst of 1981. Lewis said the movie didn't hang well, and he looked terrible in it. But the good news is that I'm in it, albeit a couple of seconds worth, and if you're interested in putting me in another movie, don't hesitate to get in touch with my agent. (Big smile)

## THE CROWD

The club was humming right along, and the crowds were steady, especially during the spring break from early March until mid or late April when the college kids from all over the country would be in Florida for the sun and the fun.

Of course, we always had extra security to help keep the kids under control because we could be sure many Stuck in Stupid things would happen during the spring breaks.

Many kids came from up north and New York, Chicago, Boston, Philadelphia, and New Jersey. Some were from families that were very much connected and were used to acting the part of the "Do you know who my Daddy is" crowd. Stu was fantastic at pointing them out, so the security would, in most cases, cut them a little slack.

## TEACHING ANOTHER ROULEAU LESSON

I was making my rounds in the club, and I went into the men's washroom and started talking to the restroom attendant and doing a little shadowboxing with him. I told him I had to get back to work and began to walk out of the restroom when I heard this sound in the back of me.

Some big goon kid said to the attendant, "If that guy bothers you again, let me know, and I will straighten him out real fast." My ears perked up like Rodger Rabbit, and I decided it would be an excellent time to establish my territory and let him and his crew know that "I don't play that game," I waited until he came out on the main floor so I could get the maximum effect across to him and his friends.

He saw me coming his way and started to give me this mean look that I guess I was supposed to be intimidated by, and when he got close, I put him on his knees and bitch slapped him in from of all his boys from New York. This action was a lesson in humility and to remind his friends that pushing your weight around in the club was not an option.

Later that night, after I left the Limelight, I went to a club down the street that was a known hangout for many wise guys. So who was sitting a couple of tables across from me? You got it, my bitch slap boy. He was with two other guys, and they started giving me the evil eye. Of course, being of sound mind and not giving a dam, I lifted my beer bottle and acknowledged them. I called for another beer and noticed the biggest of the three was heading to the restroom, so I figured it was time to get to work and establish who was on first. This guy was combing his hair, and I saddled beside him and started to comb my hair with excess water on the comb.

Every time I put water on the comb, I would make a point to flick some on this guy, surprisingly, he didn't say a word, and he left the washroom, and he and the other two were gone when I came out. So I had the feeling that they knew I was not to be fooled with, and if it was action they were looking for, I was right there to accommodate their wishes.

The next day Peter called me aside and was unhappy with my midnight performance. He was concerned that a sit-down might be forthcoming. I told him I was not sitting down with anyone for any reason, and he walked away, shaking his head. I never heard anything about it; Stu stepped in and explained that the kid was out of line.

# GAYS ARE WELCOME

Gatien understood that the audience was part of the show. There was no excitement if only straight, yuppie kids filled the dance floor. The lineup was like a cattle call in the movies. One of us would walk the line picking out interesting-looking people. Peter wanted a good "mix," and he usually got it—full credit to Peter for recognizing this vital facet of disco success.

The Gay community loved the place, and when the club changed to the Limelight, we inherited a few significant contracts that included huge and spectacular events like nothing I had ever seen before. They came in what appeared to be convoys of stretch limousines lined up at the front door and across the main parking lot along North Federal Highway.

The performers were men dressed as women in star-studded gowns with hair and makeup, turning them into gorgeous Hollywood-looking Divas. Many regular customers knew the most popular "gals" as they exited their vehicles. Each time a limo would stop at the entrance to let out its passengers, the crowd went wild.

They came from all over the United States and Canada to be here for these events. The Hollywood lights were swaying back and forth in the front of the building, and the paparazzi's cameras were constantly flashing with the entrance of each celebrity. The gay world knew most of these stars, and they played and acknowledged every cheer and wave of the crowd. The pageantry and beauty were comparable to a Broadway production and reminded me of the red carpet ceremonies at the Oscars.

# THE VALENTINO ROOM

The Valentino Room was our private restaurant with stringent dress code requirements. It was an Italian restaurant and catered to a particular clientele of Italians. So there were a lot of pinky rings on manicured hands and the traditional kiss on each cheek greeting as the "Boys" enjoyed themselves.

Handpicked bartenders were brought in directly from up north and had unique handles. For instance, the main bartender's name was "Wiggles," and his partner was just regular old "Howie." These two knew the entire clientele, and if you weren't a frequent guest or were not a friend of someone who was a regular, the bartenders asked them to leave.

# A DEADLY INCIDENT

One night when the restaurant was humming, this guy walked in and stood beside a customer sitting alone at the bar. The visitor pulled out a gun, placed it beside the sitting customer's head, and yelled, "I did this and that to your mother last night. I slapped her around, and you're a stupid son of a bitch. If you make one move, I'm going to blow your fucking head off." This verbal attack went on for about 10 minutes, and the entire room fell silent while most of the male customers held their breath and slowly reached into their jackets with obvious intent. If necessary, they would gun the mutt down in a heartbeat.

As this happened, one of our men walked in the door, saw what was taking place, and started pulling his gun out. Suddenly "Wiggles" shook his head and signaled to put the gun away and back off. The man doing the yelling turned away and walked out the door. The place calmed down, and everyone returned to their meals, but there were murmurs and glancing from table to table. There were a lot of unhappy people. Most took personal affront that anyone would enter their environment and pull a gun on one of their friends. This event was going to be a problem, and it was.

About two weeks later, during the afternoon when the place was closed, the same troublemaker was sitting at the bar when two giant monsters entered the building and immediately yanked the guy off the bar stool and proceeded to give him a terrible beating. Both assailants proceeded to stab him all over his body with swift and deadly knife thrusts. With blood flowing all over the place and him pleading for mercy, the stabbing continued until he fell to the floor and wasn't making any more sounds or movement.

They told one of our guys to clean up the mess as they wiped their hands off and calmly walked out the door.

Staff members dragged the wounded man out the back door and threw him beside a dumpster. Someone called the police and paramedics, who rushed him to the hospital. The victim did not die, but his ordeal was not over. A couple of weeks later, when the guy finally got out of the hospital, police found him with a bullet hole in his head. In those days, the Miami area was mob-orientated and could be extremely dangerous. Minding your own business was a prerequisite to staying healthy.

# COVER CHARGE

There was a daily cover change, and when we had live entertainment, the amount increased depending on the band that the club hired. A cashier at the door took the money and quickly stamped the patron's hand, for the idea was to get them in the club and spend money as soon as possible.

Andy asked me if it was a regular practice for some of those handling the money to skim some for themselves. I don't believe this happened at the door, for there were too many eyes, and Stu was in charge up there, and no one would dare take a chance of getting caught. However, I do recall the head maître D, who manipulated the system. We would charge extra, typically $100.00, for a table near the stage during a show. But our maître D would work the line outside and inevitably find someone desperate to get a front-row table. After filling up the front row, he would go out and work the line. He'd tell the customer outside that the price had risen to $150 due to high demand. If the person agreed, he would walk them up to the front and regretfully announce to the patron already sitting there that he could no longer have his particular spot because of some deal that was out of his control. He would return their $100 and seat the new customer. Then, of course, he would pocket the extra $50. This routine was an inside joke; I didn't learn of his scam till years later.

On the nights of double shows, security would quickly usher the first crowd out the door, followed by the cleaning staff making the showroom presentable. So, there was no sitting around. Instead, we had people lined up outside, patiently waiting to get in for the next show.

## LOCAL COMPLAINTS

A resident group complained to the city that Limelight patrons were parking on their property, vandalizing cars, and apartments, leaving trash, and sometimes having sex in plain sight. Their wish list involved the city forcing the club to close at 2 AM rather than 6 AM with the idea the chaos would calm down earlier. Well, this wasn't going to happen.

The club's general manager publicly blew off the complaints indicating that parking was a problem the city had to handle. That earned the ire of a Miami Herald editorial and wasn't the club's best P.R. move.

Adding to the confusion were local businesses hiring private towing contractors to clear their lots of unwanted vehicles. If a car didn't have a particular windshield sticker, the tow guy would swoop in, and the car would disappear. Patrons of the club would come out with their rides nowhere in sight. They were not happy. We started valet parking and added more men working with the valet parking guys to keep things under control. "Freddy," the manager would send one of the men out to the homes of the most vocal locals and offer them free tickets to the show. Eventually, the neighbors accepted the inconvenience of having a nightclub that wasn't going away in their neighborhood.

## DRUGS

During this time in Florida, cocaine and other illegal drugs were readily available, unlike the avalanche that overtook the state later. I don't believe we had active drug dealing in the Limelight. Kids may have been using while dancing, but they were obtaining their fix elsewhere. At that time, alcohol was the drug of choice. We were highly vigilant to any drug activity on the property, and Peter's zero-tolerance drug policy was always rigorous.

## OFF TIME

To wind down, after closing at 6:00 AM, bartenders Tommy Dinardo and Tommy "Buckaroo" Buckley and I would often go to a cabana at the beach to have a few drinks and relax. That was the extent of my personal "entertainment." I worked endlessly, grabbed food on the fly, and spent my mornings on the beach recovering. Yet, I was never exhausted, for the excitement of the light show, the driving music, and the happy dancers exhilarated me. The adrenaline rush only added to my usually tightly wound personality.

## THE RICK JAMES INCIDENT

Back at the club one night, one of the staff called me to the Valentino Room's front entrance. The security men were having a problem with one of the customers. The guy wanted to enter the restaurant, but the staff told him it was a private party, and he couldn't. However, the customer wasn't understanding, so I was called onto the scene and tried to calm him down by explaining the problem. The first thing out of his mouth was t "Do you know who I am?" I knew who he was, but I figured he was so wrapped up in himself that I would let him tell me who he was. So I politely said, "No, I don't know who you are" "I'm Rick James," he replied. Now, we regularly dealt with many wonderful celebrities, but Mr. James was a first-class pain in the ass.

Rick James was a Funk artist who put out songs like "Super Freak" and later "Mary Jane" and was very popular. However, he had many personal problems that I didn't feel were our problems, and I told him up front and personal. Unfortunately, we couldn't convince James that there was a private party and he couldn't enter. This nonsense continued for over half an hour until I finally told him he could go to the other side of the club or go somewhere else and not come back. Fortunately, after being told he had worn out his welcome, James left but was not forgotten—more on Rick James in later chapters.

## TAKING THE NIGHT TRAIN TO GEORGIA

It quickly became apparent that people with money to burn packed the area and the club during winter. But in the summer, it was a ghost town. The club would stay open until 6 AM, but sometimes, a handful of kids would wander around, and that was all there was for the night. These periods were a drain on profits. However, during the off-season, you could drive a tractor-trailer around the dance floor and not have to worry about hitting anyone. So finally, Peter Gatien decided to explore other locations and unload Limelight Hallandale. A guy out of New Jersey made an offer, and Peter decided to sell. We were on our way to Atlanta, Georgia.

# CHAPTER SIX

## THE ATLANTA LIMELIGHT
## 1979-1984

Peter Gatien, after some investigation, decided to move his operations to Atlanta to avoid the seasonal swings of attendance in Hallandale. He chose correctly. This venture would be a huge success every month of the year.

Atlanta is the capital of Georgia and had a population of approximately 500,000 in the mid-1970s. If you include the wider metropolitan area, the census showed about six million people. During the Limelight era, 50% of the residents were black, 40% white, and the remainder a mix of other races. For our purposes, it is essential to note that from around 1960, Atlanta was a progressive city with greater tolerance for gays, for example. Andrew Young, a black man, was a very popular mayor when I worked at the Limelight.

Gatien selected a former dinner theatre at the corner of Peach and Piedmont Streets in the Buckhead section of Atlanta as his new venue. We saw the last performance, which was "Fiddler on the Roof." After the play, some long-time patrons were in tears realizing their type of entertainment had ended.

We also cruised the city checking out our competition. We thought our success would be a slam dunk because we'd seen nothing that impressed our group. That thinking was perhaps arrogant, but it was correct.

Then it was a whirlwind of activity as contractors were lined up and put to work on extensive renovations. The interior design by architect Tony White was terrific. Unfortunately, but unimportantly, the building wasn't anything to look at, with a long exterior broken up by a canvas tent-like awning that protruded from the entrance. A big plus was the venue was in the back of a strip mall next to a Kroeger's grocery store. This location significantly reduced our noise complaints as we had in Florida, and there was lots of parking.

Note:
The Kroeger grocery store became affectionately known as "Disco Kroeger" since many Limelight patrons bought their munchies there.

After paying a cover charge at a booth inside the front door, patrons would follow a winding staircase down to the basement level. A stage and the DJ booth in the corner were on the right. In the middle of the room was a large dance floor with the center made of glass. At the far end, to the left, were four bars with the VIP room behind. A glass wall surrounded this section, for we wanted the crowd to be able to see the celebrities. The kitchen was in the same area, and the washrooms filled the space under the spiral staircase.

The room had incredible lighting and a tremendous sound system. In addition, there was a balcony, complete with a bar, which provided a great place to watch the action on the floor. For black and white movie buffs, we provided a cushioned tiered seating theatre complete with a popcorn machine. Finally, there were street-level offices, a coat room, and a small restaurant. It was a fabulous place!

Note:
Pictures of the exterior and interior are available. Use the Google search engine on your computer, type in "Limelight Atlanta," and when the page loads, click on "Images."

I probably visited nearly every Atlanta hotel, motel, and restaurant in preparation for our opening. I'd introduce myself to the manager and key employees like those at the front desk and the concierge staff. They would receive a VIP card that provided free entrance to our venue. Our thinking was that patrons would frequently inquire as to good entertainment locations. We never took a scientific survey about the worth of this practice, but I am confident it was helpful to the club. It was also fun for me to get to know these people, and in the future, it was nice to be recognized when I visited their businesses for a meal, for example.

The Limelight opened on January 30, 1980. It was an immediate smash hit. Famed photographer Guy D'Alema, in his book "Limelight, in a Sixtieth of a Second," described the place as "The Studio 54 of the South." Would-be patrons formed long lines outside, hoping to get the nod from patrolling doorkeepers.

Note:
Guy's book is available at Amazon.com

Controlling the door was crucial for avoiding possible trouble inside So, I and others like the fabulous Duncan Black patrolled the lines looking for potential troublemakers and making essential choices about who gained entrance. Of course, everyone had the money to get in, but Gatien smartly wanted an eclectic crowd that was important to creating excitement. Such guys like Duncan made a pile of cash each night from tips offered by would-be patrons.

Since Duncan has already put Andy in shock by relating countless "tune-ups" as we controlled the line, I might as well admit it was true. Alcohol, testosterone, and the need to impress female companions sometimes made some young males in the lineup act stupid. So, I always initially employed calm reasoning. If the guy persisted in being a jerk, we'd unload on him. There is no need to provide more detail than that at this point.

Note:
In chapter 15, Duncan describes one of our more memorable "tune-ups."

I want to mention some of the employees still in my memory. Randy "E" Easterling was a world-famous DJ, and the great Bobby Lombardi followed us up from Hallandale. Tito Acosta and Jimmy H did stints in the booth as well. Bartenders Tommy "Buckaroo" Buckley and Tommy DiNardo also came up from the Florida Limelight. I also recall bartenders Vaugh and David Manion. The club did not provide salaries for the bartenders, which created tremendous motivation for them to be fast and efficient. Their reward was handsome tips from the thirsty crowds.

Two super off-duty cops, Fulton County Deputy Sherriff Greg Lauth and Atlanta police Sergeant Carl Purdum were terrific in aiding us with security.

That reminds me of a story involving Greg and a counterfeit money incident. One night a bartender noticed a customer attempting to pass a phony $100 bill. I had security bring the culprit to my office. The mutt pulled out a gun, to my shock, and I tried to grab his arm. In a flash, Greg had his weapon out and aimed at the idiot's head. Thankfully I got the guy under control, and Greg didn't kill him. It was close!

Another tale has quickly jumped to the front of my mind. When recruiting security people, a few veteran bounty hunters put in applications. When they arrived for an interview, I discovered that most were packing a lethal 357 magnum revolver made famous by Clint Eastwood in the movie "Dirty Harry." A few of these guys were carrying two! So, naturally, we didn't allow those we took on to bring their hardware.

## CROWD

There was never any problem filling the club. We tried and succeeded in always having a diverse crowd. Openly, often flamboyant gays mixed easily with straight, middle-class whites. Some straights could also be very showy, especially when they learned this would help them gain entrance. Roughly speaking, the age range would be from 18 to 50. Despite our efforts, I am sure many underage kids made it through the door.

I enforced a dress code requiring a shirt with a collar, no hat, or torn jeans. These rules were not a problem for most of these affluent kids arrived dressed to the nines. Everyone wanted to impress everyone else.

On Sundays between 3 and 10, we reserved the clubs for gays. Of course, that didn't mean straight people couldn't come in, but we ensured they understood what was happening. These were very successful events as the gays felt comfortable in our club. They were valued, loyal, well-behaved, flamboyant customers.

During that era, cash was king. My friend Tom Good loves to tell the story of visiting the club and opening a door only to see the room stacked high with bills. The nice thing, especially for the owner(s), was that the cash kept coming like an avalanche. It was unbelievable!

## A TYPICAL DAY

I'd usually arrive at the club around noon to attend to many responsibilities as GM. For example, I would; order liquor, arrange the staffing schedule, ensure the team completed maintenance, etc. Then I'd head home to my apartment to rest, clean up, and change. By 5 PM, I was back at the club, ready to roll.

Then it was time to deal with the crowds lined up outside. After that, I would make the rounds in the club, trying to head off any potential problems at their source. Again, our efficient security staff supported me. We trained them to be polite but robust enough to move any troublemaker out the door quickly. Initially, security could summon assistance by waving a flashlight beam. Later we used walkie-talkies. Looking back, the club did not have many problems inside.

## DRUGS

Drugs were readily available in any neighborhood in Atlanta and around the country. As a result, countless people snorted cocaine, including many of our customers and staff members. But the club officially banned drug dealing and quickly evicted anyone blatantly flouting the rules. I believe we successfully kept the problem under control. Only a fool would think we could prevent drugs in the club. A kid could go outside and snort some and return.

## AIDS

Sadly, this was the era when AIDs ran rampant and decimated the gay community. I lost great friends, DJs Bob Lombardi and Bobby Anderson, to the epidemic.

## COUNTING THE CASH

During the evening, runners would collect the cash from the entrance booth every hour and take it to the main office, where a secretary would store it in a safe. Then, as the night wore down, we closed the bars one by one, taking that money to the office as well. Finally, the last bar shut off its lights at 4 AM, and all the money was in the office.

Peter Gatien and I would then start to tally the money. At first, we did it all by hand but later purchased much more efficient counting machines. Once we sorted, counted, and stacked in bundles held by elastics, it was time to head for the bank. Then, Peter and I would drive with the money but not to be stuck in stupid; we'd have a few security guards follow in another vehicle. Thankfully we never were held up, although the temptation must have been there for some of Atlanta's bad boys. Finally, if I recall correctly, I did not carry a gun on those bank runs.

## AFTER HOURS

After closing and taking care of business, many staff and I would head out to one of Atlanta's many after-hours clubs. There we'd have a few drinks and wind down from the hectic evening. Then I head to my apartment to clean up and catch some shut-eye.

Andy asked me if I had gotten worn out. No. I was wired every day and couldn't wait to get to work. I drank alcohol and abused it now and then but never on the job. Nor did I ever use drugs of any kind, which remains true to this day. I loved my job!

## MARRIAGE #2

I'm not proud to say I had another marriage failure. what follows is an abbreviated version of the 20 years we spent together.

One day while working the front door, a man I casually knew from a restaurant I occasionally ate in arrived. A stunningly beautiful lady of Cuban heritage accompanied him. Wow!

It wasn't long before Marta and I were lovers. So, was it moral to date a married woman? Probably not, but I challenged any male reader passing a negative judgment on my behavior to face the same dilemma. She was so gorgeous I'll bet 90% of you would have succumbed to temptation.

I had no thoughts of marrying again as we dated, but she did after obtaining a divorce. Consequently, we developed this routine where I'd flip a coin. If she picked the winning flip, we'd get married. I used some sleight of hand to postpone marriage as long as possible.

Then one night, I got hammered, flipped the coin, and was on my way to the alter. We got married in a very upscale restaurant, and Moe Gatien was gracious enough to act as my best man. Eventually, we had two girls whom I adore. Unfortunately, the marriage went south after 20 years, and we divorced. I wish her happiness in the future.

## THE LIMELIGHT DECLINES

Around mid-1983, our boss Peter Gatien, decided to challenge the Big Apple. My wife and I traveled up there but jointly agreed that New York City was not where we wanted to raise our kids. So, I returned to the Limelight, which Maurice Gatien, Peter's older brother, now controlled.

Maurice had been a successful lawyer in his Cornwall hometown but sought more significant challenges. Towards the end of 1982, he moved his family to Atlanta and joined the club's management. Somewhere in here, younger brother Mark Gatien also came on board.

Cubs have a short life span because their fan base is fickle and moves when trends change. To combat this, Moe shifted gears and attempted to attract middle-of-the-road customers. The slow decline continued. Let me emphasize that it wasn't Moe's fault. His strengths were different than Peter's, and I guess the slow end would still have happened under Peter's watch. It was time for me to move on. I left as Executive Vice President after starting as General Manager.

Note:
The Atlanta Limelight closed on September 26, 1987.


## CONCLUSION

The Atlanta Limelight era was one of the best experiences of my life. I am grateful for the opportunities provided to me by the Gatien brothers and wish them all a successful and happy future. Along the way, I made life-long friends, enjoyed great excitement, and loved the daily adrenaline rush. I regret somewhat not accompanying Peter to New York but had to put family first. I now entered the underbelly of the American entertainment business. That grimy tale begins in the next chapter.

FABIAN with LIMELIGHT'S BRIAN ROULEAU

Rock Star Fabrian and Brian Photo courtesy of Guy D'Alema

Movie Star Ann Margaret and Brian Photo
courtesy of Guy D'Alema

Comic Rip Thorn and Brian Photo courtesy of Guy D'Alema

Legendary singer Eartha Kitt and Brian
Photo courtesy of Guy D'Alema

Brian and racing superstar Mario Andretti
Photo courtesy of Guy D'Alema

Andy and Brian Photo courtesy of John Dickey

Brian on the cover of Us Magazine (Gag photo)

Brian in his prime in the 1980s Photo courtesy of Guy D'Alema

Brian, a security guard, and TV personality Jayne
Kennedy Photo courtesy of Guy D'Alema

Superstar musician Issac Hayes and Brian
Photo courtesy of Guy D'Alema

The Atlanta Limelight dance floor and lights
Photo courtesy of Guy D'Alema

Famous TV personality Miss Miller and Brian
Photo courtesy of Guy D'Alema

Superstar singer Tina Turner and Brian
Photo courtesy of Guy D'Alema

Brian, sister Joan, and brother Pat Photo taken by Mrs. Rouleau

Brian and cult icon Andy Warhol Photo courtesy of Guy D'Alema

Brian in US Army Uniform

**Insert for Guy D'Alema**

Entertainment and celebrity photographer Guy D'Alema has been capturing images that have been published around the world in international publications for over 40 years. He began his relationship with the Atlanta Limelight in March of 1981, the night of the club's First Anniversary Party.

During his first year as the Limelight's Paparazzi, he captured a photo of singer/conservative activist Anita Bryant dancing with known Gay Evangelist, Russ McCraw on the eve of the Atlanta Gay Right's March. The photo went around the world because of MS Bryant's vocal stance against the Gay lifestyle. That image was picked-up by the Associated Press and was his first AP World-Wide Photo Release. It appeared on the front page of the Atlanta Journal, and in the pages of Newsweek Magazine, Playboy Magazine and over 750 domestic newspapers and 7 European publications, resulting in Club Owner Peter Gatien referring to that single photo, that helped to launch his club on the international scene, as "The photo seen around the world".

Guy remained photographing and documenting the celebrities, events, patrons and crew for over 4 years before setting his sights on a move to the film and television industries.

His first film as the still photographer to capture marketing/promotional images was "Love Potion #9". For over the past 35 years, he has been capturing images on sets both in the States and overseas.

He has published a coffee table book featuring images from his years at the Atlanta Limelight entitled "Limelight...in a sixtieth of a second" (available at Amazon).

# CHAPTER SEVEN

## THE ATLANTA ADULT CLUB YEARS

Imagine walking down a brightly lit street in the finest clothes. A happy, loyal group of friends surrounds you, and excitement is everywhere. Available are great vehicles, beautiful homes, and five-star restaurants. As you move along, the group constantly runs into attractive celebrities who talk and perform. It's a dream come true, but sadly, dreams end.

Now, alone, you take a sharp left turn into a dark alley—both male and female predators pack the space. With money in hand, the males desire to watch and perhaps engage in sex. The females don't want loveless sex but will manipulate all males' weaknesses to obtain money. They are great actors and can create a fantasy world of sexual glamor. But, unfortunately, it's all a sham, gritty, grimy, and devoid of love and compassion.

I am not proud of my years in adult entertainment, but I am not ashamed of it either. The desire to earn enough money to continue the luxury lifestyle I was living took me to that milieu. Unfortunately, that work cost me a marriage and lots of heartaches. In hindsight, I wish I had been able to follow Peter Gatien to New York. But regretfully, that was not possible. Fortunately, I was physically and mentally more than tough enough to deal with the strip club predators. As Gloria Gaynor sang, "I will survive."

## BILL HAGOOD

Bill Hagood was a tough, hedonistic man who began his strip club empire in Kenosha, Wisconsin, followed by a place in Florida, then Atlanta. The latter club started at Peach and Eighth Street, but police and public pressure forced his landlord to evict the club. Hagood fought the decision in court but lost. He then moved to an old auto dealership at 887 Spring Street. I worked at this location.

I met Hagood at his big home dominated by mirrors in the interior. His practice was to intimidate people into asserting his dominance. This cheap tactic didn't work on me, and he never tried it again. Hagood offered me the executive vice president job with an $85,000 salary (Worth about $386,000 in 2022) plus a new car to run the Cheetah. I accepted on the condition it was clear that I was in charge, and I didn't want him interfering in any way. He didn't.

Note
That first year I was given a $100,000 bonus.

Hagood was a tough man who often embarrassed those accompanying him. In addition, he had no filter, and he and his wife were sexually degenerate, often using dancers from the club for their sexual pleasure. But, in fairness, Hagood traveled first class and always paid his bills. When he passed on October 27, 2020, he left a fortune to his kids.

## THE CHEETAH

As you entered the enormous rectangular room, a sexy lady sitting in a booth took your $5 cover charge with a smile. To the left was a bar with a small stage in front and two other duplicate setups flanked on either side of the room. At the far end was a more significant platform with a runway projecting out. Tables and chairs filled the rest of the space.

We had about 140 dancers and would have to run weekly auditions to keep the ranks full. Contrary to mythology, these were not college girls working their way through school, although a few were. Most were working-class women under 30, often dropped off at the club by husbands or boyfriends. It isn't easy to imagine that these males loved their partners but more likely saw them as a money machine.

Surprisingly, many dancers were not beautiful, although some were truly stunning. All of them, primarily average in looks but with good figures, used makeup, wigs, and proactive clothing to transform themselves into sexual beauties.

I recall one incident where a young dancer suddenly fled the stage and hid behind a bar. She had spotted her father enter the club, and he had NO idea what she was doing for a living.

The club did not pay the women; they were independent contractors. So, they had to pay to perform by kicking back a portion of their tips to management and the bartenders. Some dancers gave their predator male companion about $1,000 a week in cash. A rough estimate would have about 25% of the dancers addicted to cocaine. No parent would wish this kind of life for their daughter.

I was lucky; the Cheetah did not have one of those infamous VIP rooms where paid sex was the norm So, I guess that Hagood was content with the cash flow without the room, plus this situation also presented a cleaner image that kept the politicians and church groups at bay. Later, Major Herman Griner of the Georgia State Police said, "None of these places are perfect, but to my knowledge, the Cheetah is clean."

One of my great satisfactions is that I never had sexual relations with any of the girls. First, I was married, and secondly, it's not a turn-on to think of having sex with someone who has served five guys before you. Gross!

I kept my relationship with all employees professionally, and unlike at the Limelight, I did not make any good friends. It was strictly business.

In 1979, Hagood, in an attempt to prevent police pressure, issued a 14-page booklet with various rules. For example, the dancers were not allowed to squat, bend, or fondle themselves. If any dancer violated a rule and someone complained, Hagood could claim this act was an exception, and he'd plunk the rule book on the table. It was always a cat- and-mouse game with the authorities. You can be sure Hagood's lawyers got rich.

## THE CUSTOMERS

The vast majority of our customers were white men, although periodically, a girlfriend or wife accompanied their man. In addition, many of our visitors were in town to attend a convention. Atlanta had the busiest airport in the world, and conventions were huge. Our busiest nights were when the annual Baptist convention was in town. Some of these religious mutts were total hypocrites.

## EMBARRASSMENT

One day Hagood told me to round up $10,000 in cash and then accompany him to the campaign office of Mayor Maynard Jackson. As we set off, I could smell liquor on his breath and thought this venture was not starting well. I was correct.

I walked through the crowd to the mayor at the busy campaign office. I introduced myself and said I was from the Cheetah Club and we had a $10,000 donation for his run for office. Jackson graciously declined the offer explaining that he could not accept money from the adult industry for it would alienate the rest of his supporters. I indicated that I understood, and as I departed, I told Jackson to call on us if we could help in any other way.

On the way out, Hagood asked me what the mayor had said. When I explained it to him, he exploded. He was not used to being denied. Hagood verbally savaged Jackson using vile racial epitaphs, much to the crowd's shock. I was hugely embarrassed. Hagood's volatility was wearing me out.

## DEPARTURE

After two years of working with the volcanic Hagood, it was time to leave. I handed in my resignation and the required two-week notice to his secretary. When Hagood received the news, he went nuts and told the secretary to tell me I should leave immediately. He later attempted to talk me out of my decision to no avail. Afterward, he must have called me 15 more times, but there was no going back.

## SPELLBOUND

After leaving the Cheetah, a friend put me in contact with a group of New York entrepreneurs. They were interested in running an entrainment nightclub that could seat 500-1000 patrons and insisted that money was not a problem. It's not worth describing this venture in detail other than telling a few stories.

One of the main guys was Tony, and the other we called Lester the Molester. I recall still famous drag queen Ru Paul appearing as well as Jerry Lee Lewis and the Trammps with their big hit, "Disco Inferno." These two mutts embezzled money from their Japanese investors. Someone killed Tony on a trip to Japan, whereas another person whacked Lester in New York. What a pair!

Note:
I was briefly involved in some other nightclubs, but they are not worth mentioning.

## THE ORLANDO ADVENTURE

I accepted a position as executive vice president for Central Florida and ran several nightclubs, including JJ Whispers in Orlando. Stupidly I purchased a gorgeous expensive home there before getting all my ducks in order. Then, to my shock, I read a negative story about the state of JJ Whisper's finances in a paper. These events took place in 1987.

JJ Whispers was a massive facility more than four times the size of the Aardvark in Cornwall. It had a showcase room where Las Vegas-type shows appeared. In addition, there was a disco, a restaurant, and a space for gambling with all the Vegas-type games. Comedians, directly from the Letterman and Carson shows, made regular appearances. It was an awe-inspiring facility and was the place to go in Orlando.

With some concern, I meet the leading players in their office at JJ Whispers. When I asked them about the newspaper story about possible bankruptcy, they finally admitted they owed for radio ads, 25 magazine ads, billboards, taxes, and many contractor bills! Due to my extensive nightclub experience, these guys had hired me to bail them out. It wasn't what I had signed up for, but now it was too late.

I tried negotiating deals with the creditors, some of whom accepted they would never get all their money, and others threatened court action. Finally, I met with the owners and their flunkies in Jacksonville. I recall the accountant was named Bill, for he always wore a big belt buckle with his name on it. The long and the short of the meeting was that I told them to take their place and.... It was time to move on yet again. I sold the home and returned to Atlanta. These were not happy times.

## THE TAJ MAHAL

The Taj Mahal adult club owner in Marietta, Georgia, offered me a job as executive vice president. This place was colossal, covering 22,000 square feet. A massive stage at one end was too large and didn't project into the audience. On the floor were two bars, and on either wall flanking the entrance were four stores that sold things like women's lingerie, etc. The architect located a barbershop in a corner near the stage. It even had a pool outside. Incredibly between 150 to 200 girls performed every day!

When I met with the owner, he asked me what it would take to bring me on board. I replied that $2,000 a week in cash would be a start. Then I added that he would have to stay out of my way while I ran things. He agreed, and it was back to the daily grind yet again.

Within 90 days, I tripled the club's business. One of the fundamental changes was my use of a mailing list. Part of it came from the Cheetah, and our questionnaires at the front door added others. So we mailed out free entrance passes all over the country, and from their use, we could tell it was a good strategy.

As I described earlier, everything about a strip club is about separating the men from their money. Many patrons wanted to impress the girls that they were well off. We preyed on this weakness by offering bottles of Dom Perignon and Chrystal from $150 to $500 a pop. If a waitress delivered a bottle to the patron and his now attached dancer, a couple of other entertainers would rush over, faking excitement about how they'd also love a glass. The sucker's ego would always fall for the scam, and soon the bottle would be dry. Then, of course, he'd order another one.

Meanwhile, the dancers emptied their glasses into a plant stand so they could repeat the exercise without getting hammered. The club sold a lot of costly liquor that went to waste. We also sold high-end cigars, and a server would wheel around a cart and sell shots of cognac like Louis 15.

To create an image of success for those passing by, I told the parking guys to park the most expensive vehicles in the front where they were visible from the street. We used under-table lighting, makeup, and other tricks to make the dancers look much more glamorous than they were.

It was all make-believe, and the "show" pulled money out of the pockets of males at a terrific pace.

We had a VIP room upstairs. Consequently, patron could be with a woman for anything from companionship to a lap dance to complete sexual intercourse. The latter was not supposed to occur, but everyone knew it happened. Some ambitious dancers were highly active, perhaps entertaining up to five men a day. About 20% of our customers would visit the VIP room. In the principal room, dancers appeared topless and bottomless, and their garter belts made a perfect place for the stream of tips from panting customers. All dancers shared their tips with other employees.

As always, I had lots of energy and constantly changed things so customers wouldn't get bored. But there was no satisfaction in the process, it was just a job but one paying big bucks.

# THE BLACK CLUBS

At some point, a friend introduced me to a nephew of Mayor Andrew Young (1982-1990). His buddy ran about six or seven small strip clubs his employees were ripping off. The owner couldn't call the cops, for everyone knew he too ran countless scams out of the joints. He needed my muscle and experience to get things in line. Stuck in stupid, I agreed.

This milieu of six different strip clubs was a whole other world. Potential violence was simmering just under the surface all the time. Our clientele were not college kids or conventioneers out for some excitement. Instead, we had drug dealers, members of street gangs, burglars, pimps, and assorted other low-life characters. Everyone was on the hustle, and there was money all around. The trouble was that each predator wanted to take the cash from someone else. Consequently, nearly everyone was packing a gun.

Did I always carry a gun? No. Did I sometimes have a gun? Yes. Did I ever use my weapon? I'll take the fifth on that. For non-American readers, I should explain that the US Constitution, in its Fifth Amendment, reads that a person does not have to answer a question if they feel the answer may tend to incriminate them.

Knowing many of our potential customers carried weapons, we had to establish an airport-type security system at the door. So we had a hand scanner, those big arches that one walked through, and employees who would pat the customer down and go through the bags of female clients.

I wasn't stupid enough to believe no one could get a gun in the joint. However, a delivery man or the maintenance staff could accomplish that if someone waved enough cash before their face. Thankfully we didn't have any shootings in the club during my watch. But we did have some nasty business.

One day I got a call from a manager excitedly telling me the place had an armed robbery. I rushed over to find a bunch of employees milling around, and someone explained that the bad guys got away with between $25,000 to $50,000 in cash! Right away, I smelled a rat. This robbery had to be an inside job, and it was. Three managers were in on it, but when I explained the situation, the owner refused to call the cops or even fine them! He had far too much to hide, what with his skimming off the profits, his selling stolen goods in the place, and turning a blind eye to drug dealing. Later he used these mutts to torch the strip club of a predator. Unfortunately, he was ratted out and did prison time.

In another incident, two security guards became involved in a dispute outside one of the clubs. This situation wasn't like the Limelight, where a few punches settled most dustups. As I described above, the milieu was a different kettle of fish. Some mutts gunned down our guys and fled, and the cops could never find them. The fact that everyone refused to talk greatly hindered their efforts.

Then there was the sad case of one of our parking attendants. He accidentally gave the keys to a car to the wrong person, who quickly drove off. When the actual owner emerged and discovered what had happened, he was beyond furious. It turns out he had stashed a considerable amount of cocaine in the trunk, and now it was gone. In his fury, he fired a couple of rounds into the parking guy's chest and was gone. The kid had no chance and was dead.

For me, the worst was yet to come. As I explained, everyone in these joints was on the hustle. First, two dancers got stupid and ripped off some guys of their money and bling. Then, stupidly, they returned to their homes in the projects and bragged about their deed. Later the cops found their bodies dumped in the street. The bad guys had tortured them, including pulling out their fingernails before firing shots into their heads. This event was gruesome and again illustrated the world I was living in.

I felt compelled to show the company flag at the funeral. It occurred in a black neighborhood, and I was the only white guy in the church. They must have thought I was a cop and a stupid one at that. When the pastor asked if anyone wanted to say a kind word about the victims, no one dared speak up, fearing the killer's wrath. This life was a different world, as I've said previously.

## DEPARTURE

I was never afraid during this era, but that may reflect more on my stupidity than anything else. Moving between the six clubs in black neighborhoods didn't intimidate me at all, for I was confident in my abilities to run the joints and project an image of a person no one should fool with. So I could do the required job, but there was no joy or satisfaction in it. It was time to move on again.

My ex-brother-in-law suggested I contact Joe Gilardi in Florida. He ran a nationwide chain of strip clubs and was always looking for good supervisors. A new adventure was about to begin.

# CHAPTER EIGHT

## ADULT ENTERTAINMENT IN TAMPA FLORIDA

Jack Gilardi was a rough-and-tumble guy with a string of strip clubs from Las Vegas to Florida and Atlanta. Due to his personality and his company's methods to keep the cash flow coming, Gilardi was often in the news. A friend suggested I call Bobby Venero, Gilardi's top guy in Florida, as I was looking for a change and wanted out of Atlanta.

I traveled to Tampa, toured the seven clubs, and liked what I saw. They were doing a booming business, and the facilities and atmosphere were a cut way above my last stop in Atlanta. So I agreed to become an executive director of operations for Galardi South Enterprises.

Two of the clubs did not serve alcohol. At first glance, you might think this would be pretty tame, but you'd be wrong. The cover charge was $10, so the patron got to sit down and watch the most degrading porn films on the ten screens that lined the room. It was gross, but the joints were packed. In addition, those two no-liquor clubs had beds in the back rooms. This situation was far too evident, and I ordered them out.

Three facilities, the Gold Rush, the Pony Tail, and the Pink Pony, were high-end clubs with excellent facilities and an upscale clientele. Each location had standard VIP rooms where patrons would pay for various illegal sex acts, but everyone turned a blind eye to those activities. These clubs took in vast amounts of money, cash, or credit card charges.

My job was to go into these places, assess the problems, then fix them. So, for example, I might have to fire managers and then find replacements.

Sometimes I would suggest changes in staffing rules so the club could become more efficient. I always had ideas for using their security personnel to ensure the clients were safe and treated fairly.

I passed on all these suggestions and orders to the managers, and it was their job to implement them. However, my personality was such that none of them tried to buck my authority.

One change I recall was to prevent employees from borrowing from a club's float. (Money to start the day.) In truth, most borrowers would repay the loan, but this was too loose an operation and had the potential for trouble.

# RAIDS

The cops usually raided the clubs at least once a month. The authorities usually looked for signs of prostitution and any other municipal violations. The joke was that many in the raiding party were also our customers. As you can imagine, Galardi South Enterprises engaged in endless legal battles as various politicians tried to shut down these unbelievably lucrative operations.

# MY DAILY SCHEDULE

This job was not a challenge, either physically or mentally. I could have done it with my eyes closed. That, of course, also means that I was not excited about my job but loved the big bucks.

Usually, my day would start around 8 AM. Using a master key, I would visit each club, open the safe, count the money, and ensure everything balanced. Then I would take the entire haul to corporate headquarters, where a secretary would put the cash and credit card receipts in a safe.

You won't be surprised to read that the office staff also shredded all the books. I wonder why? (Sarcasm)

I would also complete many other tasks, such as checking the dancer count to ensure every club had a full complement. Maintenance was a big concern, too; I would check with each manager to ensure they arranged for tradespeople to keep the clubs looking tremendous and the toilets running correctly. I would drop into the clubs unannounced at all hours to keep everyone on their toes. My work days were at least ten hours long, but there were no shortcuts to getting the job done correctly.

# CUSTOMERS

Our customers were rough people with few social graces. They were not very polite to the servers or the dancers. I believe most of them wanted to project an image of toughness which was often a facade. They would range in age from 20 to 70, with the older group being in the minority. Money was king in the clubs, so these mutts began to think cash could bring them anything they wanted. It was dog eat dog in there with tension always present.

# BARTENDERS

Most of the bartenders were good-looking, scantily-clad women. They had to be fast and courteous, even to the most loathsome customers. Fortunately, they would share in the tops earned by the dancers. Many of these ladies turned out to be good, trustworthy employees. Unfortunately, a few were crooks and constantly verbally dueling with other ladies.

# THE DANCERS

At the time, the dancers did not require a permit in Florida. Therefore, any female could come in off the street and audition. However, I quickly learned that some of them were from up north and were looking for a way to pay for a two or three-week vacation in the sun. Therefore, there was always a changeover among the female performers.

The company knew about the VIP room, understood what took place there, and recognized that the money generated played a significant role in keeping top dancers in the club. The girls using the VIP room would kick back money to the manager, who would ensure the girl was not bothered while in action. Thus there was no incentive for the manager to enforce the law. Instead, they would encourage customers to take advantage of the delights available. Money was king.

On average, we would have 150-200 dancers performing daily. 20 to 30% of the customers would pay for a table dance. 10 to 15% would pay for sex in the VIP room. The ladies drew the men into the club, which made money from the cover charge and liquor sales. Since all the dancers were independent contractors, there were no salaries to pay. The dancers had to pay the club for the right to perform. These places produced vast profits.

## BRIBERY

All the strip clubs in Tampa were constantly under political and police pressure. So a reasonable question would be whether I was aware of any local cops or politicians' bribery in conjunction with our clubs. The answer is no, but I suppose it was possible. If so, it was taking place at a level far above me.

## DRUGS

Florida was awash with cocaine. You could get it anywhere, and many did. I am sure many of our employees and customers used the drug but not openly in the club. Did they snort in a bathroom stall? Probably. Did the dancers use it discretely in their dressing room? Probably. If security saw any evidence of open use or attempted sales, they would clamp down quickly. The club didn't need any problem with the drug cops, and they didn't make their money from drugs.

## MY LIFE OUTSIDE THE CLUB

I bought a three-bedroom condo in Tampa that was very nice. Later a beautiful huge mansion came up for sale, and I grabbed it. I would dine at upscale restaurants three or four times a week, and the cost was no consideration, for I was making a ton of money. You always believe the good times will never end. Stuck in Stupid applies here too.

One of the mistakes I made was inviting the managers and staff to a party at my home at Christmas. It was a gorgeous place with a big, autographed phone of the Sopranos TV cast and a large pool table. In hindsight, I realize this display of wealth created jealousy and envy in some employees. Unfortunately, I probably let my desire to impress cloud my thinking in this case. I didn't do it again.

## THE END

By December of 2003, things were going well. I was making loads of money, had a beautiful home and great clothes, dined in the best restaurants, and could do my job efficiently. After that, however, storm clouds were gathering. Public pressure against strip clubs had built up, so the politicians felt compelled to act.

The local cops raided four Galardi clubs and arrested four of my managers and me. They charged us with knowing sex took place in our clubs and that money exchanged hands. This problem was manageable. While the company quickly bailed us out, they just as promptly washed their hands of all of us. Galardi and his paid flunkies insisted to the press that they had no idea sex was taking place and blamed it all on the managers and me. It was a total lie, and even the authorities knew it.

Thankfully, after some time, we pled guilty to a charge, and the judge sentenced me to community service. It was no big deal, a bit embarrassing but the lasting hurt was how the company treated my managers. Galardi et al. fired the group leaving us to fund our defense on our own. Again, it was no problem for me, but it was for the other guys. Their response to the crisis was cowardly. They threw us under the bus and walked away.

I feared the state might confiscate my home and condo between my arrest and guilty plea, so I sold them both and moved back to Atlanta. A new chapter in my life was beginning yet again.

# CHAPTER NINE

## THE BIG EASY

New Orleans was once the key city in a gigantic 828,000 square mile territory running north through the middle of America to the Canadian border. This area belonged to France, but by 1803, Emperor Napoleon was in financial trouble. Consequently, he sold the faraway possession for an incredible $15,000,000, which is still only $393,000,000 today. Because of its French heritage, the oldest part of New Orleans is still called the French Quarter. I soon was a resident there.

When I returned to Atlanta from Tampa, I met a wealthy family interested in franchising three of their restaurants; Fire of Brazil, Checkered Parrot, and Jalapeno Charlies. Initially, my responsibility was to send out information to my many contacts around the south. But when they started thinking about a facility in New Orleans, the father insisted that it would only work if I took over things there. I agreed to go.

The ground floor of a hotel was the first location. There had been a previous tenant, and some fabulous artwork still adorned the walls. I thought the place had great potential.

This restaurant, Fire of Brazil, was unique. First, there was a great salad bar, all-you-can-eat, loaded with top-of-the-line foods, including shrimp. Second, servers dressed as gauchos (Skilled horsemen from South America) came to your table when you displayed the red side of a card lying on each table. You chose between 10 or 12 types of meat, at which point the waiter would slice very thin pieces from a huge slab. You could have as much meat as you wanted. On special days we featured alligator and elk. (Gag-AP) All this for around $50!

## CUSTOMERS

Conventioneers were our primary customers, but there were many tourists as well—most used credit cards, which significantly cut down any chance for employees to skim. The pharmaceutical giants also came to the Big Easy and spared no expense by purchasing cases of wine. If there were any leftovers, they couldn't be bothered hauling them away, so we put them back into the refrigerator and made a 100% profit.

## MY RESPONSIBILITIES

One of my jobs was to order wine, beer, liquor, soda, food, and all sorts of cleaning items. In addition, I had to hire and fire the personnel. Many were legal, Spanish-speaking excellent people. But on one occasion, the owner's son thought it would be cool to employ a bunch of Russians. What a disaster! This bunch couldn't fill a water glass without spilling it all over the customers.

For some odd reason, this owner's son had a unique way of talking with the staff. Some were perfectly bilingual, but most just spoke basic English. So, the son would gather the team together and speak in a booming voice, for he believed they would better understand his instructions by talking louder. Duh!

## CHECKERED PARROT

Our corporation ran another facility just around the corner from the first. It was a sports bar called the Checkered Parrot and had the required bank of TVs on the walls around the perimeter. It was on the lower floor of a 14-story Holiday Inn. I had a lovely suite on the top floor for an unbelievable $25 daily.

This facility did not depend on the convention trade but catered to the thousands of tourists who filled the streets of the French Quarter. In addition, many customers from cruise ships stayed at the Holiday Inn and required breakfast before starting their day. That meant we were open at 7 AM, and there would already be 150 hungry customers lined up.

These crowds were composed of people of all kinds of nationalities, which frequently caused a problem. For example, a customer would attempt to give the waitress his order, but neither could understand the other because both parties only had a basic knowledge of English. So I finally told the hotel they would have to provide interpreters. So they did, but that didn't end all the problems.

One day a mouthy vacationer was creating a big fuss and attempting to bully the staff. Since no one could understand the man, they called over the interpreter, but he still was wailing away. Subsequently, they called me in my suite, and I came down. I quickly determined the guy was a mutt and asked the interpreter to tell the guy to exit the premises or I'd throw him through a window. Stunned, the interpreter protested that she couldn't do that, so I quickly got in the mutt's face and threatened him. I'm sure he had no idea what my words meant, but he certainly got the drift from my demeanor and the tone of my voice. He left at a trot.

## BOURBON STREET

I don't know where to begin describing this raucous street. During Mardi Gras, the place is out of control. Drugs and liquor are everywhere. With all their bling and wild clothes, drug dealers push their products, and hundreds of hookers offer their services in the open. As is tradition, some female revelers lift their shirts to reveal their boobs and receive cheap necklaces. It is wild and a must-see if you like that sort of action. Readers can be sure Andy will never go near the place! (Big smile)

## CORNWALL VISITORS

Periodically people from Cornwall would be in the area, and it was always lovely to meet someone from home. So what follows is a New Orleans experience as related by Jean Larkin to Andy's wife, Patti.

I and three friends from Cambridge, Ontario, Sandy Dunmore, Vera Hansford, and Jessie, traveled to New Orleans for a week of fun. Unfortunately, our room at the Holiday in wasn't ready yet, so we settled at a table at the attached Checkered Parrot sports bar. After a bottle of wine or two, we became rowdy, and this big man came over to ask what the commotion was all about. He asked us where we were from, and three replied Cambridge, Ontario, but when I said Cornwall, his interest picked up immediately. He responded that he was also from Cornwall. Of course, we were positive he was giving us a line.

However, when the man began rhyming off a list of Cornwall names, including Claude McIntosh, I knew he was telling the truth and seemed to be a lovely person. Our room became available, and Brian took care of the bill as we left. We were pleasantly surprised.

The next day we went to the Checkered Parrot for lunch, and Brian was there again. The other ladies thought he was a total wildman as he talked to us. Then Brian put on a show by going over and mopping the floor. It was hilarious and transparent that this was the first time he had used a mop! Once again, Brian picked up the tab.

Before we departed, Brian told us he had another restaurant, Fire of Brazil, nearby and we should go there for supper. He then gave each of us a $50 coupon for our meal. Naturally, we were suspicious this was a con, but to our great pleasure, when we walked into the restaurant, there he was again.

Brian sat with us at the table and told fantastic stories about his life. He said the coupons would pay for their meals, but they would have to pick up the bill for the drinks, which we were more than happy to do. But when it came time to pay, there was no bill, again! To our surprise, Brian also took us on a kitchen tour, which we enjoyed because it was unlike any we'd ever seen. Thanks to Brian, our time in New Orleans was terrific.

My friends initially thought Brian was a braggart but found his stories fascinating and that he was a truly unique character. They said they were taking me on all their trips if someone continued to treat us like that.

I should note that my husband Paul and I ran into Brian on another trip to New Orleans, and I was pleased that he remembered me and that Paul got to meet him. The same happened in Cornwall at the "Wing" on Water Street. Brian came strolling in with Claude McIntosh (He was slumming. AP), and once again, Brian knew who I was. What a great personality.

(Brian's reaction to the story: "My face should be red from all that praise, but I love it.")

I also recall another occasion when a father from Cornwall called me asking if I could be a safety net for his young daughter who would be visiting New Orleans. Naturally, of course, I readily agreed, especially since this person was a good friend of my buddy Byron Gallinger. I only saw the lady briefly when she had breakfast at our restaurant, but I was available if needed.

On another occasion I hosted the beautiful Julie MacIntosh and one of her female buddies. Andy says I should let Julie tell her own story so it follows.

In 2010 I along with my friend Gwen Sutherland visited New Orleans for what was planned as a four-day trip.

A few weeks before we left my husband introduced me to Brian who was in Cornwall and holding court at Winners Sports Bar. He mentioned to Brian that I and a friend planned on visiting the Big Easy.

The Cat volunteered to book a room at the Holiday Inn in the French Quarter, adjacent to the Checkered Parrot Bar that he owned and operated. He picked us up at the airport.

Brian was a gracious host/tour guide. He took care of everything, which included picking up the bill at the high-end Morgan's Restaurant, and acted as our de facto bodyguard. while visiting (several times) the French Quarter.

The night before we were to leave, Brian brandished a print-out of the weather forecast and announced, "You guys aren't going anywhere tomorrow." The weather report said that the East Coast was being blasted by a snow storm and that included Philadelphia where we were flying for a connecting flight to Canada. So, with no flights to Philadelphia, our four-day visit turned into a seven-day stay, which had a positive spin.

The next day just happened to be February 7 and the New Orleans Saints were playing in the Super Bowl in Miami. The Saint's victory over the Colts set off one of the biggest parties New Orleans had ever seen.

And we got front-row seats - literally at the Checkered Parrot Super Bowl party with Brian playing host - to the biggest street parties we had ever seen, or will ever see again. It was a blast.

Gwen, who hadn't met Brian before arriving in New Orleans, was amazed at his hospitality and how protective he was of two gals from small-town Canada.

Thank you, Brian, for one of our most memorable ventures that launched a lifetime friendship.


# THE END

In time events beyond our control ended my adventures in the Big Easy. The hotel in which the Fire of Brazil went bankrupt, and we could not afford to wait until new owners emerged, so we shut it down. Not long afterward, the owners of the Holliday Inn, where the Checkered Parrot operated, sold to the Windium Hotel chain. They had some ideas that didn't mess with ours. We do not need to outline the proposed changes, but we insisted that the hotel must pay for them. In the end, we parted ways, and the Checkered Parrot was no more.


# A NEW VENTURE. NOT!

A seemingly wealthy man named Mark Morad approached me about obtaining a Checkered Parrot franchise for a three-story building he owned in New Orleans. He had a huge mansion and a dock worth at least $300,000 but with no boat. At the restaurant, 64 taps of beer would be on each of the two floors, with the third level reserved for refrigeration and other storage. They offered me $2,000 a week, so I agreed to take on this project, which would be no problem in normal circumstances.

I was shocked at the chaos at the facility. Morad had placed a relative in charge of the renovations, and this mutt had no idea what he was doing. For instance, the critical elevator shaft was crooked, and the lift could not ascend or descend. The whole thing was a mess, but worse was yet to come.

On May 9, 2013, a federal grand jury in New Orleans indicted Morad and others for Medicare fraud. It charged Morad with conspiracy to commit healthcare fraud and to receive and pay healthcare kickbacks. The indictment alleged he and his companies looted about $56 million from the federal Medicare program. Wow! In 2014 Morad pled guilty to conspiracy to commit health care fraud and falsifying records in a federal investigation.

I never got caught up in the fed's net, for I had no role or knowledge of Morad's scams, plus my contract listed me as a consultant, not an employee. Another page turned, and I was off to Atlanta again.

# CHAPTER TEN

## ROULEAU STORIES ONE

### RICK "NASH" KALIL

Santorini, Greece
1950s story

OMG! It was so long ago! We were just kids, 12, maybe 13 years old. There were five of us as friends: Myself, Bobby Whitaker, Jimmy Riley (Of Riley's Bakery fame), Barry Wood, and Brian. The latter two mutts lived on Pitt Street, up many stairs above the old Zellers store.

Every Saturday morning, we'd all meet at Riley's Bakery, where Mr. Riley would treat us to milk and donuts. Then my Dad would treat us to a four-hour western marathon at the Palace Theater. Brian would take charge and move us to the front of the line. Who the hell was going to argue with him? He was an aggressive 12-year-old who always acted as our bodyguard. Even the big, fat cop in charge of crowd control feared him. "Step aside, folks, here comes the "Cat!"

## GUY POIRIER

Toronto
Mid 1960s story

It s a St. Lawrence High School evening dance in the mid-1960s. The event was in the gym with a good crowd in attendance. You could go out into the back hallway and make your way to an exit that led to the track and football field. I noticed a group of people milling about outside in the parking lot. There was Brian at the start of a shoving match with two greasers who were not from our school. The fight started with two against Brian, and I heard someone say, "What's going on here?". It is legendary strong man, football star Barry Doyle. He takes in the situation and says, "That is two against one; that's not fair." So Doyle grabs one of the guys in a bear hug, immobilizing him. Brian took hold of the remaining guy and banged his head against a car several times. Finally, the guy stopped fighting, held his head, and cried, "That hurts, that hurts..."

## DR. HOWARD STIDWILL

Chicago
1959 story

I remember Brian giving an oration in the schoolyard once. He yelled, "Friends, Romans, Countrymen, lend me your ears so I can make ear soup!" He must have picked up the saying somewhere. Please don't ask me how I remembered the story, but I do. Drop that on Rouleau!

## THE LATE GREAT BIG MIKE HEENAN

The Cornwall Navy Club
1956 story

Big Mike and Rouleau are at the "Fresh Air Camp" run by principal Creighton Anderson for less advantaged kids. Unfortunately, Brian stuck a fork in the back of someone Mike couldn't recall. Anderson immediately sent Big Mike and Brian home.

## JOHN DICKEY

Country Esquire
Late 1950s story

Dickey recalls seeing a pack of street mutts surrounding the ruins of the Salvation Army Citadel on First Street near Pitt in Cornwall. Brian is up in the bell tower, hurling insults and challenges down to the howling mob, firing an endless stream of rocks at our defiant hero. Unfortunately, the passage of time and John's lack of brain power prevents us from learning the battle's conclusion. However, Brian is still around, so he survived the assault.

## JACKIE MCCLELLAN

Lacrosse great
Early 1960s story

My earliest memory of Brian Rouleau comes from the after-school dance show on Cornwall's short-lived CJSS TV. Brian was the star of the show with his super dance moves and calm demeanor. I wish I knew who his female partners were.

## EDDIE UPSON

Sea Cadet, bagpipe expert
Early 1960s story

I met Brian in grade school, and he became one of my best friends. We joined the Sea Cadets and played in a competition band. We traveled all over, competing with other bands. I recall when the group leader, Mr. "Pop" Smith, had Brian dress up as a Hula dancer with a grass skirt and coconuts, and we surrounded him playing our instruments. It got quite a laugh. Brian was very talented at any instrument. I remember him playing "Cherry Pink and Apple Blossom White" on the trumpet, which is very hard to do. He mostly played the bass drum.

We were in high school together, and I recall one day in gym class when Brian had a weight over his head when a bully from Long Sault tried to pull his shorts down. A fight broke out, and I got involved in helping Brian. Then the teacher walked in! We thought he would have us expelled, but he took our side. Later, at sixteen, we left the Sea Cadets. A lot of us, including Brian, joined the SDG Pipe Band. Again, Brian played the base drum.

Later I learned that Brian had signed up with the US Marines (The US Army). The next time I saw him, I was with my son in a restaurant. Brian tapped me on the shoulder, and I couldn't believe how muscular he had gotten. I heard later that he was a bouncer at a hotel. Then someone told me Brian opened a hotel in the US. I have seen Brian from time to time when he comes to Cornwall. He is a good friend.

## RONNIE CARTER

Deceased
The story told years ago

I worked as the bartender in the Brass Bed Lounge at the Aardvark in Cornwall in the mid-1970s. One day a big guy came storming through the lounge loudly demanding to know where Rouleau was. I said he was over on the other side. (In the disco)

The customers and I heard some shouting and banging then the mutt came limping through the lounge with a torn shirt and blood all over his face. As he left, I yelled out, "Did you find him?" to which everyone went nuts laughing.

## ANONYMOUS

Location Undisclosed
A mid-1970s story

I was young, single, and full of testosterone as I cruised down Eleventh Street in my rusty bucket of bolts whale of a vehicle. Suddenly I spied a gorgeous, sexy, short woman with big breasts hitchhiking. Without any prompting from me, my well-trained car immediately made a right turn to the curb.

The woman jumped in and quickly began talking in an amicable and flirtatious manner. Believe it or not, we ended up at my apartment, and I had the most amazing sex ever! I was smitten and couldn't wait to see her again.

After a few days of thinking little of anything but her and our sex, we had a second session in bed. It was wilder and better than the first time. She was pretty, fun, and fantastic. How lucky could a guy get? We met a third time, and again the sex was terrific. I staggered around exhausted all day, but it was worth it. I couldn't wait to be in her arms again.

I was shocked the fourth time we were together. The bombshell revealed that rough sex was a turn-on and would like it if I slapped and pretended to rape her. Reluctantly, I told her I was not comfortable with that sexual role-playing. To my relief, she said it was ok then proceeded to ravish me within an inch of my life. As I lay there totally content, she casually mentioned that she had a regular boyfriend! That revelation startled me, but I thought at least it wasn't a husband. I then asked her who the guy was. Oh my God! She told me it was Brian Rouleau! My heart and mind raced, and my stomach was on the verge of upchucking its contents. In a flash, I got dressed, ran out the door, and roared away in my car.

In a panic, I raced over to Andy Petepiece's home. He is a quiet, unassuming guy but a powerful athlete that no one fooled with. Andy told me to calm down and proclaimed he had no fear of the dreaded Rouleau. Somewhat mollified, I slunk away and kept a low-profile expecting Rouleau to show up at any minute. Thankfully he didn't, and my fear gradually subsided over a year. It was lucky Rouleau never confronted me, for I learned that Andy was afraid of his shadow and got nervous when a green light turned red.

Recently I learned that the sensational creature was still living in Cornwall. Instantly memories of fantastic sex filled my head. In addition, I briefly contemplated the possibility of hooking up with her again. Then I recalled that Rouleau came home every summer and was still as formidable as ever. My sexual fantasies evaporated in the blink of an eye, and I drove on a wiser man.


## RONNIE PRICE

Cornwall


Brian and I have been lifetime friends, as were our mothers when they were alive. During that time, Brian and I had many "adventures," but I will share only one. Here it is.

Brian and I live on the corner of Water and Amelia Street in our early teens. We would walk to Central Public Elementary School and then to CCVS when we entered high school. One day we were headed to CCVS when we heard that a guy named Red was selling his 1951 Holman car. In short order, we bought the thing for $30!

I don't recall how we got it home, but we parked it on the side of the road and spent hours sitting in it discussing how we would use the Holman. Owning this machine was a big deal for us. At first, we agreed not to drive it on the street. But, oops! Temptation got the best of us. We decided to take it to CCVS the next day but only once.

In the morning, we set off early. Brian was a year older, so he was behind the wheel. We proceeded west on Water, then turned north on Sydney. All was going well, and we were proud of ourselves. What were the chances things could go wrong? We were in for a big surprise.

At the corner of Sydney and Fourth was a four-way stop. We pulled up, and then---a cop car came to a halt to our left. We were in shock. The decision was made to act cool and proceed north on Sydney. Brian waved to the cop to proceed. Instead of driving ahead, the officer waved at Brian to go. This slapstick act went on about three times! Finally, Brian, with his foot shaking like a leaf, bumped our way across the intersection and up Sydney.

Unfortunately, the cop followed us up Sydney and pulled us over halfway up the block. I told Brian he was going to jail, but he replied that he didn't think that would happen and to leave everything to him. The policeman walked up to the side door and said, "Young man, may I see your license, proof of ownership, and insurance?" We were stunned!

Brian had no license, but we had the ownership but no insurance. Rec had also given us a receipt for the $30 cost of the vehicle. By this time, students gathered around while the officer returned to his cruiser to check on things through his radio. It seemed he took a long time, but in reality, he probably was gone only for a few minutes. Unfortunately, he didn't have good news.

"Here's the deal, fellows," he solemnly said. "This car is not worth the fines I can give you. Driving without a license, failing to change ownership, and having no proof of insurance violations add up quickly. Just sign the registration, and I will have a tow truck take it to an impound lot. Its final destination will be the scrap yard. "We were stunned but had no choice but to agree. We stood on the sidewalk and watched the wrecker tow our dream away.

Brian and I are now old with 75 years of history. I love Brian like a brother because he has always been in my life. Brian has a big heart and is always loyal to his friends. At the end of any conversation, Brian always says, "I love you, brother." The feeling is mutual. It has always been so and will always be the same.


## DUNCAN BLACK

Limelight Security
Mid 1970s story

I worked at a bar across from the street from the Limelight. Each night I looked on in amazement as Rouleau worked the long line of customers. In his sharp clothes and lots of bling, Brian dominated the line and periodically made attitude adjustments on those who dared to challenge him. I wanted to be just like Brian.

Fortunately, the Limelight hired me to work security, so I immediately copied Brian in everything from dress, attitude, and mannerisms. Soon everyone assumed we were brothers. I liked that.

I admired Brian for he was always fair but never backed down from a challenge, no matter the opponent's size. I quickly learned that Brian would always have my back despite the number of adversaries. I believed in Brian, and he never let me down.

As a doorman, you received a lot of tips from would-be patrons in the line hoping to get in the doors. One day Brian heard me bragging about my good fortune and quietly pulled me aside. He said, "Duncan, there is no need to brag; just feel lucky you are doing well." He was right.

I should add that I wore "The Brian Rouleau Starter Kit." That meant I had many rings, bracelets, a big watch, and layers of gold hanging around my neck. At the time, I believed I looked very cool. However, that similarity in bling to Brian's contributed to the next problem.

While standing out front of the club, this big guy starts staggering toward me. Blood was all over his face, and his clothes were torn and tattered. He looked as if he had gone through a meat grinder. He began yelling at me as to why I beat him up. What?

Just then, Brian exited the front entrance adjusting his tie. He approached and asked, "What's going on?" The guy responded that I beat him badly and he wanted satisfaction. Brian apologized and began to rebuke me mercilessly. Finally, Brian told the guy that he would take me inside and fire me. The poor beat-up mutt expressed satisfaction and shuffled away.

The real story was that Brian pounded the guy out and threw him in a dumpster. The Rouleau went inside to change his bloody clothes. When the guy approached me at the door, he believed I was Brian and thus was very hostile. However, when Brian returned, he played the innocent and defused the situation. This guy was tough and clever at the same time.

## DUNCAN BLACK STORY TWO

I am working the door at the Atlanta Limelight when these two big guys approach the door with drinks in their hands, planning on leaving. The club had promised the city we would eliminate drinking outside to decrease rowdiness. So, I politely explained the rule and offered to call a cab. I figured that was the end of the little problem. But no! These two clowns attempted to sneak out with their drinks.

Brian and I approached them in the street, and Brian quietly explained the rule again. They responded with verbal aggression and even grabbed the collar of my expensive sports jacket. One of them aggressively said, "You may call the cops and have us put in jail for a day, but we'll put you guys in the hospital."

To this challenge, Brian responded, "Oh, is that so, lad?" Then we laid into them in a fury. Andy won't let me provide the gory details, but it's safe to say one ended up with a broken leg and the other with a caved-in head.

When the cops arrived, we explained that one guy fell off the curb and broke his leg while I punched the other guy, and my ring cut up his head.

The officers took us uptown for paperwork, and then the magistrate released us for an appearance in court in the morning.

Being stuck in stupid, Brian and I didn't go home to clean up and sleep. So instead, we hit the after-hours club and got wasted. Then, before the court appearance, we showered and wore fresh clothes but sober we were not.

Someone pushed in one guy in a wheelchair with a cast on one leg. The doctors had shaved the other mutt bald so they could tend to the massive gash on his head. They then stapled up the wound, making him look like a movie monster. What a sight!

These kinds of dustups happened a couple of times a week. We were in a combat zone every day. I could relate many more incidents, but Andy is afraid the readers will think we are animals.

I admire and respect Brian and learned a lot about life from him. Brian is a dear friend.


## ANDY PETEPIECE

From the boondocks
Story from 1979


Most readers are unaware that I am a respected mafia researcher, writer, and consultant. In addition, a select few friends know that I also tend to perform incredibly heroic violence in defense of the weak. I've decided to reveal one example of this trait in the book.

It was May 3, 1979, and I was driving down Montreal Road in my $600,000 Ferrari. Suddenly, to my left, I noticed Brian in a brawl with four large mutts who had attempted to rob a little old lady of her groceries. I immediately braked to a halt and ran over to the scene.

The first guy was a monster, probably 6 feet 4 inches and about 280 pounds. I lifted him above my head and tossed him over a pickup. A second jerk attacked me with a knife but using my karate skills, I parried his blow and knocked him into coocoo land with a thundering right hand. Meanwhile, the Cat leveled the third loser with a flurry of blows that left him lying on the ground, spurting blood everywhere and moaning like a baby.

Then the desperate fourth hood pulled out a .357 revolver and pegged a shot at me. Fortunately, the slug bounced off my steel-like bicep and into the bushes. Rouleau grabbed the weapon, twisted it into a pretzel then hammered the guy with tremendous blows. He then tossed the poor soul into the rear of a passing garbage truck.

We were triumphant, and a group of adoring females quickly surrounded us. Then the gorgeous Lynda McDonald burst through the crowd and threw herself in my arms, proclaiming I was her hero. Then she planted a long kiss on my welcoming lips. I was in heaven!

Suddenly I felt someone slapping my face. It was my fantastic wife, Patti. She said I had yet another of my frequent fantasy hero dreams and needed to take my anti-delusion pill. I slunk off to the bathroom where she indicated that my bubble bath was ready and that she had put my favorite rubber ducky in the water. Then, it was back to reality and my boring life.

# SUSAN

Story for the early 1960s

Hi Margot.... here are a couple of things I remember about Brian, aka "The Cat" ..... although in those days he was still "A Kitten"...lol

I always thought of him as a protector of us girls. If any guy harassed us, our response was.... I'm telling Brian so you better watch out!

He was a very talented musician, there wasn't an instrument he couldn't play & excelled on the trumpet & drums. He always looked so handsome marching in the parades in his Sea Cadet (???) uniform playing the trumpet or drums.

He was a great dancer, (I taught him everything I knew). We practiced our dancing in the kitchen of the house on 3rd Street where I lived (under the watchful eye of my dad!) We won many dance contests…the Twist & the Jitterbug…at St Columban's on a Saturday night. I wish I still had those little plastic trophies!

I remember a bunch of us were on the porch of someone's house & someone dared me to drink some vinegar…. I was sitting on the railing, drank the vinegar & went ass over tea kettle…. within seconds "The Kitten" (who grew up to be The Cat) was there to pick me up.

At Central Public School he was a prankster & a bit of a shit disturber. Anything to raise the blood pressure of the nasty Mrs. Crothers.

Over the years, our lives went in different directions & we lost touch. However, Brian will always have a special place in my heart & will always be my friend.

Susan

# CHAPTER ELEVEN

## ROULEAU STORIES TWO

### GUY D'ALEMA

Atlanta Limelight Celebrity Photographer
A World Renown talent

Limelight had a policy of taking any visiting celebrity to city hall, where the mayor would present them with the city's keys to creating publicity and goodwill. Usually, things went smoothly, but in the instance I will relate, they didn't. Nevertheless, it still makes Brian and I laugh today.

For many decades Miss Miller was a regular audience member on the Tonight Show, the Merv Griffin Show, and others. She became a minor celebrity, and everyone recognized her. So the Limelight invited her to Atlanta to host parties hoping her fame would attract attention to the club. It did. As was the practice, we took Miss Miller to city hall to meet the mayor.

Andrew Young had a small area in his office with an easy chair, a sofa, and lights appropriate for photos and filming. On this day, media crews packed the office due to the quirkiness of this celebrity. First, Mayor Young greeted Miss Miller and directed her toward the couch. But instead, the feisty old lady headed for the easy chair, which was Young's regular perch.

Young quickly pointed out that she should sit on the couch, which was very comfortable. Miss Miller replied that if it was so great, the mayor should sit there and promptly plunked down on the easy chair. The media loved the awkwardness and her total lack of respect for his authority. The Limelight PR people cringed with embarrassment.

Trying to find a connection, the mayor asked Miss Miller if she saw his appearance on Merv Griffen. Her reply startled the mayor and the media. She said he was never on that show, for she was in the audience at tapings. He replied that she must have been away that day, but Miss Miller rejected that possibility. It made for another awkward moment.

Things only got worse with Mayor Young presented the old lady with a certificate and the keys to the city. Again, she stunned everyone by proclaiming she could not accept the paperwork. Shocked yet again, the mayor asked why? Miss Miller said they had put down Mrs. Miller.

Embarrassed, Mayor Young muttered that they would fix up a new certificate, but she could hold on to the incorrect one in the meantime. To this suggestion, the incredible lady asked why she'd bother keeping the one with the mistake and handed the paper back to the stunned mayor.

The visit was a disaster for the mayor and the club's PR people but a goldmine for the media.

Next, it was off to a local radio station. As Miss Miller and the host sat and patiently waited for the technicians to get everything in order, Miss Miller asked the PR guy. "How about a bump?" The host was confused and asked if there was a problem. The PR guy quickly responded that there wasn't. and Miss Miller wanted her seat cushions plumbed up a little. Hearing this, Miss Miller said, "That's not what I mean." Confusion and embarrassment reigned. In truth, the old lady was a regular cocaine user and wanted a "bump" before the interview began.

## GUY D'ALEMA STORY TWO

One evening the Limelight featured a performance by a troop of dancing girls like New York's Rockets. They arrived in three limousines, and Brian greeted the occupants of them one by one. The first two vehicles had left when the last pulled up to the entrance. Brian peered in the window, then turned to me and said, "Watch this." He let three women out, then closed the car door and turned away from it.

A black man exited the limo as Brian turned to face him. It was a famous disco star, Rick James, with wild hair. Rouleau says, "Where the f... do you think you are going?" The startled James replied that he was with the dancing group. Rouleau responded, "Not tonight," and blocked James's path to the club. An enraged James shouted, "Do you know who I am?"

The Cat cooly replied, "Yeah, you're the mutt who stiffed me at our club in Hallandale. (James left without paying his hefty bill) I told you never to stop at one of our clubs again."

James' girlfriend came running over, wondering what was going on. After the singer explained the situation, his lady friend said, "Well, I guess you might as well go back to the hotel." A humbled James asked her to return with him, but she declined and said she would have a great time with the other ladies. The Cat had what I could describe as a "Cheshire Grin" on his face. Payback time!

## GUY D'ALEMA'S STORY THREE

Anita Bryant was a former Miss America who retained her fame many years later. But unfortunately, her very conservative Christian religious beliefs caused her to condemn gays openly. That made her a hero in some circles and an object of scorn in others.

To everyone's shock, Brian learned that Anita Bryant would arrive at the Limelight. Of course, this action was entirely out of character, for everyone knew gays frequented the club and were welcome. It was also Gay Pride Week, and the club expected a significant increase in their gay patrons.

Brian tipped me off about Bryant, so I rushed to the club and set about capturing her on film. I finally found the anti-gay activist on the dance floor with a tall, slender man in a white suit. I began snapping pictures, but few noticed for my flash bulbs just blended in with the disco lights.

Later I sent out my film to be developed; not sure what to expect, but I felt this was a momentous event. Eventually, I permitted American Press to publish my photo worldwide. They had discovered that Bryant's dancing partner was a well-known gay evangelist. It was a sensational event considering Bryant's fame and strident anti-gay stance. In my opinion, my picture made my career and significantly increased the notoriety of the Limelight. It was terrific for both but not so for Miss America. Few shed any tears for her embarrassment.

## MARGOT GILLARD

BC

My name is Margot Gillard, and I am originally from Cornwall. I am proud to say Brian Rouleau was a good friend in our youth and still is. Thanks to modern technology, we are still in touch. Unfortunately, I have not had the good fortune of traveling home to Cornwall recently. However, I would do so regularly in the past, especially if Brian was in town. I hope I can return to that practice in the future.

Upon one of my visits home, I was at Big Mike Heenan's Navy Cub on Sixth Street for Brian's annual "Welcome Home" party staged by Big Mike and yourself. That night, you were kind enough to visit our table to inquire who we were and how we knew Brian. We were all impressed with your interest. Thank You for the welcome.

I can't think of one particular story of Brian. Still, I can honestly say he was a friend to many, kind, with a heart bigger than his body, and a fabulous dancer with musical talent. Brian could play various instruments, and no one could twirl the drumsticks while playing the base drum in the Cornwall Sea Cadet marching band like Brian.

I'm not sure if any of this fits your ideas for the book, but I wanted you to know that Brian has all these qualities, talents, and natural gifts. I am sure many others would agree. Over the years, he continues to show his loyalty, love of people, and life each year by visiting his hometown and touching base with as many friends as possible. As successful as he has been in life through dedication and hard work, it's obvious he has never forgotten his roots and friends.

I should add that Brian is an excellent comedian and could have made a living doing that. I wish you and Brian great success with the book and will eagerly purchase a copy once it is published. Finally, might I say, if you have a friend in Brian, you have a friend FOREVER.

## MAURICE GATIEN

Cornwall lawyer
Owner of the Atlanta Limelight

In October 1982, Ann-Margret came to the Limelight in Atlanta – Brian was a big fan of hers and looked forward to her visit. She had been a performer for the US forces in Vietnam, and he admired her efforts on behalf of the troops. (note: I can't remember whether Brian had seen her when she traveled to Vietnam – as her tours there might not have coincided with his time serving there – but he was aware of her having done shows during USO tours).

One person who showed up from New York City on the same evening to take photos of Ann-Margret was photographer Ron Galella who was a paparazzi – probably the most well-known one – who had taken pictures of the rich and famous for many years (and who would continue to do so for decades afterward – he has published a book featuring his many photos – including the one at the above-noted link – which may include Brian on the right-hand margin – in the center background is one of the Limelight security staff Duncan Black, who worked with Brian).

Ron was himself an interesting character – and Brian and I enjoyed chatting with him at the front door to the Limelight on the evening in question as we waited for Ann-Margret to arrive. Ron was full of anecdotes – and he was a very genial and friendly person.

Ron explained that, within the world of celebrities, there were genuine celebrities (like Ann-Margret) who were justly famous because of their talent – and who remained nice people. Others clung to fame like a drug and sought every desperate opportunity to get publicity and to be mentioned in the press – in particular on the infamous Page 6 of the New York Post.

Sometimes, a celebrity hadn't had a hit for a while after a succession of dud movies. Sometimes, their star had faded because of age. Sometimes, they had simply been lucky for a while, and now their lack of talent was simply asserting itself.

Ron explained that, during the previous week, he'd received a call from one particular actor's wife, tipping him off that her husband (who'd been a condescending jerk toward Ron when he was a hot commodity but who was desperate for any coverage when the offers dried up) would be leaving a New York restaurant the next evening around 10 "with a woman who was not his wife" – as a piece of gossip that would held land her husband on Page 6 and maybe help his waning career. To Ron, it all sounded too staged.

It was an interesting conversation with Ron – as we chatted about the "Mythology" of celebrity news – that it happened and then got covered – and the "Reality" of celebrity news – that much of it got planted and was essentially manufactured.

It was like finding out that Wrestling was fixed.

Later that evening, after Ron and Ann-Margret had left, Brian and I talked about what it was like – back in the day, growing up in Cornwall – during an era when wrestling was dominated by such colorful characters as Killer Kowalski and Mad Dog Vachon and Whipper Billy Watson – and finding out that wrestling was fixed.

Well, not exactly fixed – just choreographed for our entertainment. We concluded that it was good to laugh and enjoy the "Show" – but not take it too seriously, since it might not always be true. Page 6 was the fiction – the reality was that some celebrities like Ann-Margret had held on to their authentic selves – and that was more valuable than the publicity.

# AL WHITTEN

Atlanta
Served in Vietnam in the Marines

I applied for a job at the new Limelight club, which was still under construction. Someone directed me to Brian, standing in an army shirt. That and a brief conversation about our lives in Vietnam told me this was a guy whom I could trust. That instinct proved to be true right up to the present day.

At first, the club put me on the door, but, unfortunately, I did not prove to be as user-friendly as they had hoped. So, after that, I spent my time cruising the lower level, where the crowd drank and danced. I wouldn't say I liked the disco music, but the facility was incredible with its lights and sound show. This location was the place to be in Atlanta, and the hordes lined up to get in.

Let me relate a story about this very irritating rich kid who was a regular patron. One night he couldn't stop complaining to me about numerous trivial matters. Finally, fed up, I told him he should talk to Brian if there were a problem.

I followed the jerk up the stairs to the upper level to see Brian. Stupidly the guy immediately began to threaten Brian. He tried intimidating Brian by claiming to have practiced Tae Kwon Do for 17 years. Meanwhile, he had gotten in close to Brian. Our leader has an imaginary "danger zone" around him, and anyone who crosses that line is taking his life into his hands. Brian responded, "Is that so? Well, I have been practicing tutti fruiti for seven years." At that, Brian launched a vicious right-handed haymaker that shattered the guy's jaw and knocked out several teeth! Man, did that ever happen quickly, but it was no surprise.

A week later, Brian answered the phone, and the caller was mumbling so much Rouleau could hardly understand him. But amazingly, it was the same mutt with his jaw all wired up by the doctors. He was desperate to be allowed back into the club; that's how popular the Limelight was back then.

I feel blessed and fortunate to have met Brian, who took me under his wing and always had my back. He remains a true and valued friend to this day. Semper Fidelis. (That is the US Marine motto which means "Always Faithful"-AP)

# REFLECTIONS

I have had a challenging life due in part to my poor upbringing and lack of the presence of my father. I survived thanks to a loving mother who made every effort she could to get us through the hard times.

I'm extremely proud of my time in the United States Army and the three years I served in Vietnam. These experiences taught me survival lessons that helped me overcome the many obstacles that have been thrown in my path.

Certainly, one of the highlights in my life was the Limelight Entertainment Complex located in Atlanta Georgia. It was a very exciting time with a constant flow of major movie actors, music stars, and famous sports celebrities. I loved the people I worked with and met. It was a fascinating time in my life

My era in the strip clubs was often unpleasant and extremely dangerous. Numerous individuals were shot dead often for some minor altercation but, it was a way of surviving financially. I also operated many upscale restaurants throughout Florida, Georgia, and Louisiana and enjoyed great nights and entertainment with extremely beautiful individuals

I wish my private life would have been happier and more successful. There was plenty of blame to go around including on my shoulders. I place the mistakes on no one but myself.

To my former wife Marta, who blessed me with two wonderful daughters, Jessica and Michelle, who are my strength and pride to this day, I thank you. and sincerely wish you happiness.

I am also so grateful for the fantastic number of loyal friends I have accumulated over the decades.

I have learned to deal with my regrets and certainly recognize my strengths and weaknesses. My standard model has always been, "I never give up."

# THE CAT

It has been an honor as my great friend Brian mentally walked me through his fascinating life. Brian stood strong with our agreement that this book would carry both the good and the bad along with introspection. During this journey, I was often unexpectedly surprised and emotional. My greatest satisfaction was discovering how many people love and admire Brian, mostly for his never-ending friendship. As the old expression goes, "If you can only have one man in the foxhole with you, The Cat would be a great choice."

With Respect and Love
Andy Petepiece

# APPENDIX A

## Some of Brian's Friends

| Alden | Alannah |
|---|---|
| Badante | Jim |
| Bazinet | Lucy |
| Bazinet | Louise |
| Begg | Ron |
| Black | Duncan |
| Boucher | Mary Ann |
| Briere | Guy |
| Briere | Jacques |
| Briere | Sue |
| Callaway | Iris |
| Caplone | Paul |
| Cardinal | Ronald |
| Cardinal | Carole |
| Carson | Tom |
| Carter | Ron |
| Chadwick | Lani |

| | |
|---|---|
| Clark | Susie |
| D'Alema | Guy |
| Desjardins | Diane |
| Dickenson | Carrie |
| Dickey | John |
| DiNardo | Suzette |
| DiNardo | Tommy |
| Edwards | Gary |
| Edwards | Doris |
| Edwards | Patti |
| Edwards | Cin |
| Edwards | Derek |
| Edwards | Rita |
| Edwards | Keith |
| Edwards | Susan |
| Edwards | Jim |
| Farber | Gerry |
| Fillion | Ernie |
| Freeman | Karin |
| Gabri | Larry |
| Gallinger | Byron |
| Gallinger | John |
| Gallinger | Mark |
| Gallinger | Alason |
| Gallinger | Lloyd |
| Gilbertson | Ashley |
| Gilbertson | Brent |
| Gilbertson | Terry |
| Gilbertson | Jason |
| Gillard | Margo |
| Givogue | Verna |
| Good | Tom |
| Gray | Keith |

| Gray | Vicki |
|---|---|
| Harrington | Bordie |
| Harrington | Brian |
| Harrington | Russ |
| Harrington | Janet |
| Hyde | Lloyd |
| Ingram | Billy |
| Kalil | Rick |
| Kyte | Phil |
| Lalonde | Bear |
| Lalonde | Gerry |
| Lalonde | Tanker |
| Lalonde | Linda |
| Lalonde | Rosalie |
| Lalonde | David |
| Larin | Sharon |
| Legault | Lynda |
| Lemire | Yvon |
| Lindle | Brian |
| Liscomb | Brian |
| MacIntosh | Claude |
| MacIntosh | Julie |
| Martel | John |
| Martel | Jacques |
| Martel | Satch |
| Martel | Donald |
| Martel | Lenard |
| McFall | Joe |
| McItee | Gib |
| McMan | Duncan |
| McNichol | Brian |
| Megenhardt | Bob |
| Megenhardt | Jackie |

| | |
|---|---|
| Moffat | Murray |
| Motard | Henry |
| Neuman | John |
| Nurse | Ian |
| Parent | Nick |
| Parent | Camille |
| Parsons | Zack |
| Phillips | Billy |
| Pommier | Rose |
| Pommier | Andre |
| Price | Billy |
| Price | Ron |
| Roy | Charlie |
| Roy | Jack |
| Roy | Pierre |
| Scotti (Brazilian Queen) | Marilia |
| Squires | Janet |
| Stone | Stu |
| Taylor | Katherine |
| Upson | Eddie |
| Witton | Al |
| Wood | Barry |
| Zerran | Jay |

# APPENDIX B

## Some of Brian's Vehicles

1951 Hillman
1968 GTX 440 High Performance
I put 5 complete sets of extra wide tires on the car in 18,000 miles leaving my
signature skid marks on almost every stop street in Cornwall.
1969 Cadillac Sedan Deville
1970 Cadillac El Dorado
1975 Cadillac Coupe DE Ville
1975 Cadillac Séville
1976 Cadillac Fleetwood
1978 Cadillac El Dorado
1980 Lincoln Continental
1981 Cadillac Bustle Trunk Diesel
1982 Lincoln Stretch Limousine
1982 360SL Mecedes Silver
1984 560SL Mecedes Candy Apple Red
2008 Cadillac Escalade
2011 Chrysler 200 Hardtop Convertible Special Edition
2023 Kia High Performance Stinger
Brian
I made a point to buy the newest, flashiest cars on the market every year.

Note One:
At least two expensive Mercedes Benz vehicles should be in that list somewhere.

Note Two:
I have included this list to demonstrate that Brian's need for attention wasn't restricted to his clothes and bling.

# APPENDIX C

## Cornwall Area Vietnam Vets

Partial List from Memory
My apologies to those I missed

| | | |
|---|---|---|
| Bobka | Terrence | US Navy |
| Caron | Gaston | US Army |
| Degan | Leo | US Navy<br>US Navy<br>Commendation |
| Herne (O'Bryne) | Kevin | US Army |
| Hill | Peter | US Army<br>169th Engineers<br>Battalion |
| Lapointe | John | US Army |
| Levac | Joseph | US Navy<br>Bronze Star |
| Pidgeon | Kenny | US Army |
| Vinet | Richard | US Army |

# APPENDIX D

## Celebrities I Met

| |
|---|
| Alabama |
| Alguire, Noel |
| Ali, Muhammad |
| Allen, Peter |
| Barry, Gene |
| Blair, Linda |
| Brown, James |
| Cole, Natale |
| Cruise, Tom |
| De Mornay, Rebecca |
| Devine |
| Durning, Charles |
| Fishburne, Lawrence |
| Gaynor, Gloria |
| Haggerty, Dan |
| Jackson, Jermaine |
| James, Rick |

| |
|---|
| Jones, Grace |
| Jones, Quincy |
| King, Evelyn "Champagne" |
| Leonard, Sugar Ray |
| Lewis, Jerry |
| Little Richard |
| Madonna |
| Margaret, Ann |
| Marry Jane Girls |
| McEnroe, John |
| McGraw, Ali |
| Mills, Stephanie |
| Miss Miller |
| Most, Donny |
| Nash, Kevin |
| Pride, Charlie |
| Reynolds, Burt |
| Ru Paul |
| Road Warriors |
| Savage, Joe |
| Silva, Henry |
| SOS Band |
| Springfield, Rick |
| Stallone, Sylvester |
| Stanley, Paul |
| Stewart, Rod |
| Summers, Donna |
| Sylvester and Two Tons of Fun |
| Taco |
| The Drifters featuring Rick Sheppard |
| The Fabulous Thunderbirds |
| The Trammps |
| The Village People |

| |
|---|
| Traveno, Lee |
| Turner, Tina |
| Tweed, Shannon |
| Ward, Anita |
| Warhol, Andy |
| West, Adam |

Manufactured by Amazon.ca
Bolton, ON

39909765R00085